The Demonic Roots of Globalism

The Demonic Roots of Globalism

by
Gary Kah

Huntington House Publishers

Huntington House Publishers
P.O. Box 53788
Lafayette, Louisiana 70505

Library of Congress Card Catalog Number
94-73606
ISBN 1-56384-087-1

Printed in the U.S.A.

Unless otherwise indicated, all Scripture
quotations are taken from the authorized
King James Version, published by The Word
Publishing Corporation.

Contents

A Note from the Author

Hope For The World has launched the publication of a regular **newsletter** to keep interested readers up-to-date on new developments concerning the matters discussed in this book. If you would like to be placed on our mailing list for such a news bulletin, please print your name and complete mailing address on a sheet of paper and enclose it, along with any suggestions or comments you might have, in an envelope addressed to:

> Gary Kah
> Hope For The World
> P.O. Box 899
> Noblesville, IN 46060-0899

Because your thoughts and input are greatly appreciated, we will make an effort to read each letter. As time permits, we will respond whenever possible to your letters; however, please understand that we have a small staff, which sometimes makes a prompt reply impossible. Also, please keep us posted of changes in your address to eliminate any delays in receiving our mailings.

As always, if you or any friends come across significant information related to the topics discussed in this book, you are encouraged to mail your information along with the appropriate documentation to the preceding address. Please highlight or underline the specific information that you would like to call to our attention. Your information could be used in future books or publications to keep the American people and Christians throughout the world informed. Although we have a network of researchers already in place, it is impossible for a few people to stay current on everything that is going on in the one world movement.

In order to save time, we will only write back if we have a question; otherwise, you may assume that your information has been received and reviewed. Thanks for your input!

===========◇===========

Introduction

Several years have now passed since the publication of my first book, *En Route To Global Occupation*, which warned America of the coming push for a one world government. As we all know, much has happened in the arena of world affairs since that time. Many of the scenarios discussed in that book are now rapidly coming to fruition. The United Nations of today, for example, is dramatically different from the U.N. of a few years ago.

Each year, it seems, new international treaties (or agreements) are being ratified, giving the U.N. more power and control over our personal lives, often at the expense of our national sovereignty and in open defiance of our U.S. Constitution. This recent "empowerment" of the United Nations will soon be felt by all of us, as new international laws and regulations finally become enforceable, taking on some real clout. A "world tax" is even being discussed as the U.N. seeks ways to fund the implementation of its new environmental and population control policies; its growing "Peacekeeping Forces"; and the huge bureaucracies being established to oversee GATT (General Agreement on Tariffs and Trade) and the newly formed World Trade Organization.

Since the release of *En Route To Global Occupation*, I have had the opportunity of traveling the country, appearing on hundreds of talk shows, while fielding questions from thousands of concerned listeners. To my surprise, the most often asked questions have pertained to spiritual matters as they relate to the coming world government. As a result this book will have a slightly different focus, as I seek to address these concerns. People close to me, aware of the fact that I was holding on to a lot of research material on New Age occultism, compiled while working on *En Route*, have repeatedly urged me to make this information available to the public, in order that people might benefit from it. I have decided to follow their advice.

Whereas my first book presented an overview of the three major areas where globalists are most influencing our lives—summarizing developments in the political, economic, and religious realms—this book will probe deeper into the so-called New Age movement, explaining the spiritual motivation lying at the heart of the New World Order.

This work presents a unique glimpse at the personal lives and beliefs of those individuals who, during the last century, have had the greatest influence in shaping the New Age movement of today; people such as Helena Blavatsky, Carl Jung, Pierre T. Chardin, Robert Muller, John Randolph Price and others. By examining these lives, the book pieces together a chronological history of the movement, while in the process pointing out the pitfalls and dangers of its empty teachings.

A special focus will be given to Alice Bailey, the founder of Lucis Trust, a mysterious but powerful organization whose occult concepts continue to influence key members of the United Nations and the Council on Foreign Relations. An entire section is devoted to exposing Bailey's anti-Semitic and anti-Christian world-view. In addition, we will look at the phenomena of spirit guides and see what the current fascination with angels is all about. The reader will also discover why there probably won't be any major changes in foreign policy in the new Congress, and why Newt Gingrich and Bob Dole seem to insist on supporting the Clinton administration's globalist views on empowering the U.N.

This book is not intended to be a voluminous, definitive study on the emerging New World religion. It is, however, designed to be a practical handbook—a supplement to *En Route*—looking more deeply at the religious underpinnings of a dangerous, but rapidly growing movement. Although this particular writing has been geared toward Christians—equipping them to take a more effective stand for their faith—this information will benefit non-Christians as well by pointing out the clear differences between biblical Christianity and the occult teachings of the New Age. It is my hope that the following pages will offer the reader useful insights while addressing some of the most often asked questions on this subject.

Chapter One

$$\diamond$$

Laying the Foundation
for
Omega Point

For other foundation can no man lay than that is laid, which is Jesus Christ.

—1 Corinthians 3:11

One can view our world and its history of the rise and fall of nations, its wars and conflicts, and its rising and ebbing of ideas and philosophies as a crazy quilt of happenstance—of unplanned, unrelated events. Or we can see in all of this a pattern, a slow moving forward of human history toward a goal, a climactic event, or as some refer to it, the "Omega Point."

There are two basic views of human history and where mankind is headed. Both are proclaiming their ideas about man, his purpose on earth and his ultimate goal. Both approaches are gaining followers, or "believers" in numbers never before imagined, and each is diametrically opposed to the other. We seem to be living in a time of polarized choices, when gray areas are fading away, and black and white are once again becoming more distinctive and clear. The time of sitting on the fence and taking life as it comes may not be an option for us in the future as it has seemed to be in the past.

Changes that affect an entire society never happen overnight, although it may seem that way to many people, especially those who take their information only from the local newspaper and television. Over a period of many decades, the foundation has been laid, one stone at a time, for a deception in the minds of men that would engulf not only this nation, but the entire world.

Something of this magnitude could not be planned or orchestrated by one person or group of persons. But, we are told in the Bible that there is a being capable of such an undertaking. His name is Lucifer. (Many New Age occultists refer to him by that name.) He was a member of God's highest order of created beings, an angelic prince, and his name means "light-bearer." Isaiah 14:12-15 and Ezekiel 28:11-19 tell us much about his character and of God's judgment upon him.

When he was cast from the mountain of God (Ezek. 28:16), he lost his high and holy position before "the Ancient of Days"; but, he lost none of his incredible, supernatural intelligence and power. It only became corrupted. His sin was in coveting God's place and desiring, as a created being, the worship that is due to the Creator, the Most High, alone (Isa. 14:13-14). When he was not able to deny God the worship given Him in heaven (by attempting to get a majority of the angels to worship him rather than God), he turned his eyes toward earth, and ever since, his desire has been to gain the worship of men.

Lucifer, who became known as Satan after his rebellion, understands our fallen human nature very well, since he is the one who sought to corrupt our originally pure and innocent nature. He doesn't need a wide variety of deceptions and lies to use on us. There are two that serve his purpose well enough.

The first is to cast doubt on God's Word, to twist and change it to mean something entirely different from what God originally intended. For example, God has promised eternal life in heaven for all who believe in His Son (John 3:16). Those who reject God, on the other hand, will be separated from Him for all eternity in hell. Satan has twisted this system of eternal rewards and punishments into the false belief that man will never die . . . that he just keeps coming back in different life forms (reincarnation), and that there is no final judgment by God!

The second tactic is to convince us that we have the right, the ability, and the power within us to become like God. Lucifer knows very well that this is no more possible for us than it was for him. Still the lie continues, and down through the ages man has continued to accept that deception in one form or another. All of this can be found in the third chapter of Genesis, along with the disastrous results for the first man and woman who believed his convincing lies.

Very few people perceive the fact that human history has been a battleground. The battle is being waged by Satan and his legions against our Creator; and the prize is our souls, and the decision in the heart of each person as to whom he will give his loyalty and worship. If any should doubt this, remember that Satan even tried to get Jesus to worship him. That was two thousand years ago. The battle is now in its final stages and mankind is consciously or unconsciously choosing his allegiance.

Satan has successfully elicited devotion to himself through the ages by introducing, through human vessels, a variety of false religions, cults and outright Satan worship. It is not my purpose here to give a detailed history of his activity in ages past, but rather to focus on developments of the past one hundred years or so, since the groundwork for the climax of this battle has been very cleverly laid over the past century. During this time, a seemingly unrelated series of events has gradually been taking place. We have already studied the developments in the political and economic world. (An overview of this information is contained in my first book, *En Route to Global Occupation.*) Now we will take a look at what related developments have been taking place in the spiritual world.

The reason this deception has crept up un-observed on so many people can best be demonstrated through the well-known analogy of the frog in the pot of water. If you put a frog in a pot of boiling water, he is smart enough to know that he is in terrible danger and will immediately jump out to safety. But if you turn up the heat very slowly, a little at a time, he doesn't notice the changes that are taking place and will slowly cook to death. Many people today are slowly cooking to death and don't seem to realize how far they have come from where they once were.

The first step in this plan to deceive human-ity was the same as the first lie told to Eve—that was to cast doubt on and twist God's Word. This has been the main activity of Lucifer in the last century and, as we shall see, he has been quite successful.

False Religions and Cults of the 1800s

In the 1820s, the seeds of a new religion began to grow into what is today known as Mor-monism. One of the beliefs of the Mormon church, as found in their book, *Pearl of Great Price*, states that "Jesus was the spirit brother of Lucifer before he entered the world."[1] Mormon-ism today is one of the fastest growing religions in the world, and is quite possibly the wealthiest (on a per capita basis).

Spiritism, on the other hand, with its empha-sis on contacting the dead (actually, contacting demonic spirit beings posing as the spirits of dead persons), became an organized religion in 1848. In our generation it has gained acceptance among many of the world's elite, being responsible for leading thousands astray by introducing them to forms of divination.

Between the years of 1860 and 1870, Mary Baker Eddy began to teach her ideas on Christian Science. Followers of this religion now believe that it is impossible to understand the Bible apart from Mrs. Eddy's teachings as found in her book, *Key to the Scriptures.* Apparently there was no point in even reading the Bible in all those previous centuries without Mrs. Eddy to enlighten us.

Theosophy had its beginning in 1875 under the leadership of Helena Petrovna Blavatsky, and later, Annie Besant. The roots of this organization run throughout the New Age movement of today. More on this later.

Jehovah's Witnesses came into being in 1879. This new religion denied the doctrine of the Trinity and the divinity of Jesus Christ, and printed its own translation of the Bible called, *The New World Translation.* Key passages in this translation have been changed to fit their teachings. Again we see the attack with the accompanying subversion of God's Word. Who in this country has not had either a well-meaning Mormon or Jehovah's Witness at their doorstep at some point, ready to share with you their "new truth."

The Unity Church was organized in 1886 under the leadership of Charles and Myrtle

Fillmore. Of the "new" religions that had their origins in the nineteenth century, the Unity Church, along with Theosophy, is probably the most representative of New Age thinking. Truly Lucifer was busy laying his foundation of deception during this period of time. But this was only the first phase. The work was just beginning.

Before we take a look at the next step of his plan, let's first take a closer look at the teachings of two of his choice instruments from the nineteenth century. The first is Helena Blavatsky, founder of the Theosophical Society.

Helena Petrovna Blavatsky

In studying the teachings of any new religion or cult, it is always wise to take a close look at the founder of that religion. One would hope to discover a life that is at least somewhat consistent with the founder's teachings. Madame Blavatsky's life seems to be a perfect match with her teachings, which are found in the volumes of material she wrote.

She has been described by her various biographers as

> having a restless and very nervous temperament, one that led her into the most unheard-of, ungirlish mischief; an attraction to, and at the same time fear of the dead; her passionate love and curiosity for everything unknown, mysterious, weird and fantastical.[2]

> From her earliest youth she attracted the attention of all with whom she came in

contact. . . . She rebelled against all discipline, recognized no master but her own good will and her personal tastes.[3]

She was one of the most evil and immoral women who ever lived . . . with personal duplicity and profound contempt for humanity.[4]

Helena Petrovna Blavatsky was born 12 August 1831 in Russia. Her mother died when she was eleven years old, and from that time on she was passed back and forth between her father and other relatives, for it seemed that no one could manage her. As her mother was dying, she was heard to comment, "Ah well! Perhaps it is best that I am dying, so at least I shall be spared seeing what befalls Helena! Of one thing I am certain, her life will not be as that of other women."[5]

As a child she was known to converse with animals and birds and to frighten the other children with terrible and captivating stories. From an early age, she demonstrated the abilities of a medium and, while in a trance, frequently saw the majestic figure of a Hindu in a white turban. She called him her protector and believed that he saved her from danger on many occasions. She later described an alleged face-to-face meeting with that same "master" in England at the age of twenty, when he instructed her to leave for India to organize the Theosophical Society.

She acquired the name Blavatsky at the age of seventeen when she married an elderly general as a result of a dare from a governess, who challenged her "to find any man who would be her husband, in view of her temper and disposition."[6] The marriage lasted three months at which time Helena deserted him and ran away to begin a life of world travel in service to "her master." Of all this she stated, "I wouldn't be a slave to God Himself, let alone any man. . . . Woman finds her happiness in the acquisition of supernatural powers. Love is but a vile dream, a nightmare."[7]

So we see that Madame Blavatsky—an immoral individual, heavily involved in the occult—was hardly a candidate to be chosen as an instrument to bring God's light and truth to mankind, but one perfectly suited to the purposes of the "great deceiver." Thus, Blavatsky drew many followers to herself and her organization during her lifetime. Her "chelas" or disciples were devoted to her and were more than willing to help spread her doctrines, many of which were acquired during her travels to Egypt and India.

Many of her beliefs can be found in two thick volumes entitled *Isis Unveiled* and her main work, *The Secret Doctrine*. This material was allegedly dictated to her through her "masters" who were called by the various names of Koot Hoomi, Morya, and simply, "The Ascended Masters of Wisdom." These "masters" were, she believed, more highly evolved souls who, after going through numerous reincarnations, had left the earth plane and were now guiding mankind.

In the New Age movement of today, automatic (demon-manipulated) writing is very popular. The names of these so-called ascended masters, or spirit guides, are often as well known as the authors themselves. "Seth," for example, writes through Jan Roberts, and the popular Ruth Montgomery books are supposedly written by her many "guides." Of course their message is always a "cosmic gospel" that is opposed to orthodox Christianity.

If we look at what the "masters" have taught the world through Theosophy, we find that they have "depersonalized God and created various planes of spiritual progression culminating in universal salvation and reconciliation through reincarnation and the wheel concept of progression, borrowed unblushingly from Buddhism."[8]

> God and man are the two phases of the one eternal life and consciousness that constitutes our universe! . . . This conception makes man a part of God, having potentially within him all the attributes and powers of the supreme being. [Author's note: This is also the core belief of pantheism, the underlying belief system of the Eastern mystery religions, including Hinduism, Buddhism, and Shintoism, among others.] It is the concept that nothing exists except God and that humanity is one portion of Him—one phase of His being. . . . If the idea of the imminence of God is sound, then man is a literal fragment of the consciousness of the Supreme Being, is an embryo-god, being destined to ultimately evolve his latent powers into perfect expression. It is the unqualified assertion that humanity is a

part of God as leaves are part of the tree, not
something a tree has created in the sense that
a man creates a machine, but something that
is an emanation of the tree and is a living
part of it. Thus only has God made man.
Humanity is a growth, a development, an emanation, an evolutionary expression of the
Supreme Being.[9]

It is difficult to understand in all of this, how
an impersonal God-force could have created beings of intelligent thought, creativity and indi-
viduality. In contrast, the Scriptures teach us
that God can speak (Acts 28:25), and that He
has a mind (Rom. 8:27). The god of Theosophy
is certainly not the God of the Bible.

If Lucifer were going to use a mortal person
as a channel to discredit the Bible and weaken
the Christian faith, what teachings would he most
want to discredit? Let's take a look at *Isis Unveiled* to see what he had to say through Madame Blavatsky.

Like Buddha and Jesus, Apollonius was the
uncompromising enemy of all outward show
of piety, all display of useless religious ceremonies and hypocrisy. If, like the Christian
Saviour, the sage of Tyana had by preference
sought the companionship of the poor and
humble; and if instead of dying comfortably,
at the age of over one hundred years of age,
he had been a voluntary martyr, proclaiming
divine truth from a cross, his blood might
have proved as efficacious for the subsequent
dissemination of spiritual doctrines as that of
the Christian Messiah.[10]

In this statement, Blavatsky brings the blood of Jesus down to the level of any martyr or founder of other religions. What a contrast we find in the twelfth chapter of Revelation where it is Jesus' blood that actually overcomes Satan.

> And the great dragon was cast out, that old serpent, called the Devil, and Satan, which deceiveth the whole world: he was cast out into the earth, and his angels were cast out with him. . . . Now is come salvation, and strength, and the kingdom of our God, and the power of his Christ: for the accuser of our brethren is cast down, which accused them before our God day and night. And they overcame him [Satan] by the blood of the Lamb, and by the word of their testimony. (Rev. 12:9–11)

The following statement appears on page ten of *Isis Unveiled*:

> How can a missionary in such circumstances meet the surprise and questions of his pupils, unless he may point to that seed and tell them what Christianity was meant to be? Unless he may show that, like all other religions, Christianity too, has had its history; that the Christianity of the nineteenth century is not the Christianity of the middle ages, and that the Christianity of the middle ages was not that of the early Councils; that the Christianity of the early Councils was not that of the Apostles and that what has been said by Christ, that alone was well said.[11]

With one swoop of the pen, Blavatsky and her "masters" do away with over two-thirds of the New Testament. The New Age movement of today strangely believes in the religion "of Jesus, not about Jesus." (New Agers believe that we can all attain the "Christ-consciousness", becoming gods ourselves.) This is not surprising. Since they want no personal God to whom they are accountable, occultists would hardly want to listen to the words of the Apostle Paul who makes such powerful admonishments as to how the Christian life should be lived. Besides that, they twist the words of Jesus to mean just the opposite of the original intent of the literal, logical statements.

Madame Blavatsky goes on to say, "Thus we may infer that the only characteristic difference between modern Christianity and the old heathen faiths is a belief of the former in a personal devil and in hell."[12] It is very difficult to fight a war if you don't know anything about the nature of the enemy. It is impossible to fight a war if you don't even believe that there is an enemy. Lucifer would like nothing better than to convince mankind that he does not exist, thus leaving him a free hand to go about his work of deception and destruction. But Jesus said, in words that cannot be twisted,

> Ye are of your father the devil, and the lusts of your father ye will do. He was a murderer from the beginning, and abode not in the truth, because there is no truth in him. When he speaketh a lie, he speaketh of his own: for he is a liar, and the father of it. (John 8:44)

It is obvious that Helena Blavatsky believed the "father of lies" and helped to spread his false light when we look at her statements in *The Secret Doctrine*, her most significant work. On page 53 she states, "Better be man, the crown of terrestrial production, and king over its opus operatum, than be lost among the will-less Spiritual Hosts in Heaven."[13] She goes on to say,

> Satan is that Angel who was proud enough to believe himself God; brave enough to buy his independence at the price of eternal suffering and torture; beautiful enough to have adored himself in full divine light; strong enough to still reign in darkness amidst agony, and to have made himself a throne out of this inextinguishable pyre . . . the prince of anarchy, served by a hierarchy of pure spirits.[14]

Madame Blavatsky, in *The Secret Doctrine*, says that Eliphos speaks with unparalleled justice and irony, when he writes: "It is this pretended hero (Satan) of tenebrous eternities, who, slanderously charged with ugliness, is decorated with horns and claws, which would fit far better his implacable tormentor."[15] She sums up her ideas on the devil as a redeemer by saying,

> And now it stands proven that Satan, or Fiery Dragon, the "Lord of Phosphorous"—brimstone was a Theological improvement—and Lucifer, or "Light-Bearer" is in us; it is our Mind, our Tempter, our Redeemer, our Intelligent Liberator and Saviour from pure animalism.[16]

Blavatsky believed she received her directions from the Enlightened Ones or Initiated Adepts (synonymous with "spirit guide" or "master"). Under "Adept" her glossary states, "He who has obtained." In occultism, an Adept is one who has reached the stage of initiation and become a master in the science of Esoteric philosophy (secret occult doctrines and practices).

One would think that these teachings of a rebellious and fanatical woman of the last century would have little bearing on the lives of people today. After all, what sane person would allow himself to be influenced by such ridiculous ideas? Probably no one completely sane would. But it is interesting to note that from his jail cell, shortly after the murder of Sen. Robert Kennedy, Sirhan Sirhan requested a book by Blavatsky entitled, *Manual for Revolution*. Blavatsky's life was lived for world revolution and the overthrow of the present social world order. In this particular book, she called for the assassination of national leaders as an instrument for world revolution.

Another well-known follower of Madame Blavatsky was Adolf Hitler. He was known to have kept a copy of *The Secret Doctrine* at his bedside. The margins were full of comments and notes in his own handwriting.

Joseph Carr, in his book, *The Twisted Cross*, makes the following insightful observation:

> The foundations of both Nazi and New Age Movement philosophy are in the occultic doctrines that were made popular in the late nineteenth century by the theosophical movement. Both Naziism and the New Age Movement

depend heavily upon the teachings of Helena
P. Blavatsy (*The Secret Doctrine* and *Isis Unveiled*). From theosophists Hitler derived his
genesis theories and the notion of a control-
ling hierarchy of initiates. Both the theosophists of the time and the Nazis believed that
mankind was guided by superior beings,
Ubermenschen (supermen), who live in re-
mote areas of the world, such as the Gobi
Desert (Western China) and the Himalayan
nation of Tibet. There was a substantial Tibetan and Chinese community in Berlin because of the occultic interests of German society, and Hitler augmented them with new
emigres after he came to power. By 1941,
there were more than one thousand Tibetans
living in Berlin.[17]

Today there are branches of the Theosophical Society and its offshoots in every major city
of the United States. Thus, the first step in the
structure that is supposed to take us through
that quantum leap in human evolution to our
Omega Point has apparently been laid.

Helena Blavatsky had many close associates
and followers in her lifetime. However, when
she died at the age of sixty, she was alone and
estranged from even her closest friends, but
remained loyal to her masters to the end.

God gives us some clues in the first chapter
of Romans as to how a human spirit can become so twisted and deceived.

> Because that, when they knew God, they glo-
> rified him not as God, neither were thankful;
> but became vain in their imaginations, and
> their foolish heart was darkened. Professing

> themselves to be wise, they became fools. . . .
> And even as they did not like to retain God
> in their knowledge, God gave them over to a
> reprobate mind, to do those things which are
> not convenient. (Rom. 1:21-22, 28)

Second Thessalonians 2:10-11 states, "They received not the love of the truth, that they might be saved. And for this cause God shall send them strong delusion, that they should believe a lie."

Unfortunately, where Madame Blavatsky's work ended, others were eager and ready to pick up the banner and carry on. The next in line for a short time was Dr. Annie Besant (1847-1933). It is interesting to note that she is listed in the *Dictionary of Mysticism and the Occult* by Nevill Drury. This dictionary describes her as

> an English theosophist and social reformer
> who became president of the Theosophical
> Society in 1891. . . . Originally an intellectual
> force rather than a spiritual one, she experi-
> enced a dramatic illumination by making con-
> tact with the Tibetan Mahatma Master Morya
> and became his disciple. . . . Dr. Besant was a
> leader in the Co-Masonic movement and a
> prolific author.[18]

There were plans to bring forth her adopted son Krishnamurti, an Indian mystic as the Messianic Leader and Reincarnation of the World Teacher. However, he declined the honor and, shortly after that, the earthly leadership to further Lucifer's plans, (via Theosophy, at least) was transferred to Alice Ann Bailey, the new president of the Theosophical Society.

Alice Ann Bailey and
The Tibetan, Djwhal Khul

Of the two people focused on in this chapter, the work of Alice Bailey is probably the most important in laying the foundation of the New Age movement. By the time she had finished her work in 1949, she had established Lucis Trust, World Goodwill (to which I have already linked the leadership of the World Constitution and Parliament Association; see *En Route to Global Occupation*, pp. 77, 83), Triangles, the Arcane School, and the New Group of World Servers; she had written twenty-four books, a total of 10,469 pages, most of which were allegedly written through her by her spirit guide, The Tibetan, Djwhal Khul. My Bible contains 972 pages. Apparently, God was able to say it all in far fewer words than the "masters."

Bailey, who as we shall see was extremely anti-Jewish and anti-Christian, was a far more powerful force to be reckoned with than most people realize or would care to admit. Lucis Trust, an organization which Bailey originally founded in the 1920s under the name Lucifer Publishing Company, today boasts a membership of approximately six thousand people. Some of the world's most renowned financial and political leaders have belonged to this organization; including individuals such as Robert McNamara, Donald Regan, Henry Kissinger, David Rockefeller, Paul Volker, and George Schultz. This is the same group of people that runs the Council on Foreign Relations, the organization responsible for founding the United Nations. It is interesting to note that Lucis Trust was headquartered at United Nations Plaza until recently.

Alice Ann Bailey was born of high social standing in Manchester, England on 6 June 1880. Although her parents both died when she was young, she wanted for nothing and was raised by relatives in a protective environment. As a young woman, she spent a number of years in Christian work. However, in reading her autobiography, one senses that she "served" the Lord without ever really "knowing" Him. It can become a tiresome experience to work in Christian service without the indwelling power of the Holy Spirit, and Alice soon burned out.

All alone in a strange country with three young daughters after a difficult and painful marriage, she was ripe for the same deceptive forces that had used Helena Blavatsky in establishing the Theosophical Society. These forces first contacted her through two English ladies, who lived in Pacific Grove, California. They came from the same social background in England as Alice and were deeply involved in the occult teachings of Theosophy.

Bitter over an abusive marriage and confused about her purpose in life, Alice began a metamorphosis which transformed her into a master teacher of the occult and one of the most receptive channels of demonic influence the world had yet known. Of this period she states,

I sat up in bed reading *The Secret Doctrine* at night and began to neglect reading my Bible, which I had been in the habit of doing . . . my mind woke up as I struggled with the presented ideas and sought to fit my own beliefs and the new concepts together . . . I discovered, first of all, that there is a great and divine Plan. . . . I found that race after race of human beings had appeared and disappeared upon our planet and that each civilization and culture had seen humanity step forward a little further upon the path of return to God. I discovered, for the second thing, that there are Those Who are responsible for the working out of the Plan and Who, step by step and stage by stage, have led mankind on down the centuries. I made the amazing discovery, amazing to me because I knew so little, that the teaching about this Path or this Plan was uniform, whether it was presented in the Occident or in the Orient, or whether it had emerged prior to the coming of Christ or afterwards. I learned that when I, in my orthodox days, talked about Christ and His Church I was really speaking of Christ and the planetary Hierarchy.[19]

Of these "orthodox" days she writes, "All this time I was steadily and forcefully preaching the old-time religion. I remained appallingly orthodox or—to use the more modern word—an unthinking Fundamentalist, for no Fundamentalist uses his mind."[20]

Lucifer and his forces don't very often find "willing" atheists through whom they can work and channel information. After all, these spirits operate in the realm of the supernatural, as does

God. True atheists don't believe in the existence of such a realm.

While Alice Bailey rejected the Christ of Calvary, she was willing to embrace a supernatural occult belief system.* This allowed her to be used for thirty years as a channel for transmitting all that the forces of darkness desired humanity to accept as truth. She died on 15 December 1949, just thirty days after "The Tibetan" had finished writing through her. Apparently, her usefulness to the hierarchy of evil was at an end.

Before we take a closer look at what these "masters" taught, we need to understand who they claimed to be and how they were able to work so effectively through a human channel.

The Ascended Masters

In their own words,

> The spiritual Hierarchy of the earth is the aggregate of those of humanity who have triumphed over matter, who have achieved the goal of self-mastery by the same path that individuals tread today. . . . They are no longer centered in the individual consciousness but have entered into the wider realization of the

---

* Technically, one could argue that only God is supernatural, with everything that God created—including angels (some of which became fallen angels)—being part of the natural realm, part of God's creation. However, for most people the term "supernatural" has widely come to be used as a direct reference "to any being or phenomena having to do with spiritual matters or relating to the spirit realm." Hence, my use of the term supernatural in this book should be understood to be synonymous with the latter definition.

planetary group life. . . . They work according
to plan and are known as "The Custodians of
the Plan."[21]

In other words, they claim to be a group of
highly evolved human beings who (having experienced the process of reincarnation) watch over
and guide the progress of humanity.

> The senior members of the Hierarchy are the
> Masters of the Wisdom. A Master of the Wis-
> dom is one who has through self-mastery
> achieved mastery over the whole field of hu-
> man evolution. Having done so, his under-
> standing is no longer limited or bounded by
> the human kingdom but also encompasses
> that kingdom of pure consciousness termed
> the kingdom of souls . . . Because of an indi-
> vidual natural predisposition to certain lines
> of work, they each have a special contribu-
> tion to make towards human progress in one
> of the seven major fields of world work: po-
> litical, religious, educational, scientific, philo-
> sophical, psychological or economic.[22]

From the state of our world today, it looks
as if they have been quite busy. However, their
success seems to be more in creating chaos than
in bringing about progress.

New Age occultists refer to these spirits by a
variety of names, including:

Spirit Guide	Hierarchy of Initiates
Guide	Spiritual Hierarchy of the
Master	Earth
Enlightened One	Planetary Hierarchy
Adept	The Hierarchy
Initiated Adept	Ubermenschen (German)
	Custodians of the Plan

As previously stated by Blavatsky, the most powerful or highest ranking members of this so-called hierarchy are known as Ascended Masters of the Wisdom. More typically they are referred to as Masters of Wisdom, Ascended Masters, the Tibetan Masters, or simply, Masters. All are references to the same thing.

The general understanding among New Agers is that these beings are humans who have gone through numerous cycles of reincarnation, evolving to a higher level of spiritual perfection each time. Some occultists believe that these creatures physically walk the earth (or have possessed those who can) and are concentrated in the region of the Himalayas—Tibet, Nepal, and western China (because this is supposedly the part of the world that has been most receptive to their occult teachings). Others believe that these "more highly evolved beings" exist only on a spiritual plane, being accessible only through occult meditation.

Regardless to which belief New Agers cling it is understood that these beings are able to communicate telepathically with those individuals who open themselves up and become receptive to their "enlightened teachings." This is accomplished by going into a trance, or an "altered state" of consciousness, which apparently gives "the masters" a license to "come through."

(My belief is that these entities are nothing more than demonic beings, fallen angels which can take on the appearance of advanced human beings to individuals who go into altered states

by practicing various forms of occult meditation.)

The most advanced occultists, such as
Blavatsky and Bailey, I believe at some point
came to the understanding that these beings
were demonic spirits, serving Lucifer. There are
too many Luciferic references in their writings
for anything else to have been the case. But
whatever explanation occultists give for the existence of these beings, they have the same
deceptive impact: They lead people away from
God's truth by causing them to accept the false
hope that "they too can overcome death and be
as gods."

Angels and Altered States

It is interesting to note that the belief in
reincarnation is particularly useful in explaining
or rationalizing the existence of these beings.
However, individuals who are not pantheists and
do not believe in reincarnation may have the
same "spiritual experiences" if they unwittingly
open themselves to the occult.

For example, an atheist who goes into an
altered state while experimenting with self-hyp-
nosis, not aware of the fact that he is involving
himself in a spiritual rather than a scientific
matter, may have a similar encounter. However,
since he does not believe in the existence of a
spirit realm, these beings are more likely to take
on the appearance of an extraterrestrial; leading him to believe that they are more highly
evolved beings from another world, who are able

to communicate in ways we are not yet able to fully understand. In fact, such an explanation would seem to be acceptable to anyone who believes in evolution and life on other planets, whether he is from an atheistic or a religious persuasion. I am personally aware of people working for NASA and the U.S. Department of Defense who claim to have had such experiences.

Those persons, on the other hand, who come from a Christian background but who repeatedly (and possibly naively) go into altered states of consciousness, may at some point be approached by beings posing as angels; or even as Mother Mary, in the case of Catholics. Such an explanation would most likely be accepted by a person with some Christian family roots, but who is personally not firmly grounded in the faith. After all, who doesn't believe in angels? (Satan's angels usually don't volunteer the fact that they are "fallen" angels.)

It would only stand to reason that Satan's angels, being spiritual entities with superior intelligence, would know where we are most vulnerable for deception and would approach us in whatever form is most acceptable to us . . . if a person repeatedly opens himself up to the occult realm via altered states/occult meditation.

It is no coincidence that books on extraterrestrials and angels (fallen angels) are typically found in the New Age/Occult section of bookstores. In fact, angels seem to be the latest craze.

As I am writing this book, America appears to be enthralled with the subject of angels. Some of the current best selling books on angels, from a New Age perspective include:

Your Guardian Angels, by Linda Georgian (from the Psychic Friends Network) and *The Angels Within Us*, by John Randolph Price (also the author of *The Superbeing*). Another book, *Mary's Message to the World*, by Annie Kirkwood, supposedly conveys Mother Mary's enlightened wisdom for humanity. It is currently extremely popular in Catholic circles.

To keep all of this in perspective, we must remember that God's holy angels exist as well, and outnumber Satan's angels two to one. However, these angels cannot be summoned whenever people wish. Rather, it is God who decides their purpose, along with when and where to send them. Unlike fallen angels, they give the glory for their deeds to God alone, not drawing attention to themselves. God's angels are invisible to the human eye, but we know by faith, according to God's Word, that they are there. (The fact that I am still alive probably bears witness to this fact.)

It should be clarified that most individuals who go into a trance do not have supernatural encounters on their first try. In fact, some people may practice occult meditation for years without having such an experience. Perhaps they have a Christian mother or distant aunt who is fervently praying for their protection and salvation. I do not know how else to account for the fact that some people have these experiences while others do not. However, based on personal testimonies, I do believe that going into an altered state dramatically increases one's chances of having a demonic encounter. I also know that it is never God's will for humans to induce an altered state.

The following diagram depicts some of the most popular techniques, including forms of occult meditations, that are presently being used for inducing altered states of consciousness. Please notice the active brain wave activity of a person in a normal, alert state of consciousness as opposed to the reduced brain activity of an individual in an altered state.

The Plan of the Hierarchy

Christ (which "the Hierarchy" considers to be an office or a position which can be attained, not the person of Jesus) is supposedly one of these ascended masters, but so is Buddha, and somehow in their scheme of things, Buddha is always a little superior. They tell us that Christ came to show us the love of God, but Buddha came to bring us enlightenment. They go out of their way to let us know that the Bible has been misinterpreted and the true meaning lost through the centuries. But somehow, this has never happened to the sacred scriptures of the East, so they can be trusted. They tell us that the teaching, planned by the Hierarchy to precede and condition the world for the New Age, also known as the Aquarian Age or the New World Order, falls into three categories:

LEVELS OF CONSCIOUSNESS

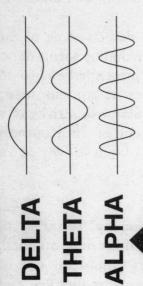

Altered-states of consciousness:

OMEGA

DELTA

THETA

ALPHA

BETA

Normal, alert consciousness:

TECHNIQUES FOR ACHIEVING ALTERED-STATES:

▲ Meditation / Centering
▲ Visualization (Including Guided Imagery & Astral Projection)
▲ YOGA
▲ TM (Transcendental Meditation)
▲ Mind Dynamics (Flotation Tanks, Cyber Vision, etc.)
▲ Parapsychology (Including Telepathy, Clairvoyance & other Psychic Phenomena)
▲ Hypnosis
▲ Mind-Altering Drugs

▲ Bio-Feedback
▲ Virtual Reality (certain programs)
▲ Silva Mind Control
▲ The Forum (Formerly Erhard Seminar Training)
▲ Arica
▲ Life-Spring
▲ Life-Stream
▲ Alpha Level Training
▲ Stress Management Seminars (One or more of the above methods are frequently taught or employed at such sessions)
▲ Martial Arts (some of the concentration/focusing techniques)

1. Preparatory, given from 1875-1890, written down by Helena Petrovna Blavatsky.

2. Intermediate, given from 1919-1949, written down by Alice Bailey.

3. Revelatory, emerging after 1975, to be revealed on a worldwide scale via the radio and television (meaning that some of the major film producers and script writers, as well as television personalities—whether they be politicians, religious leaders or merely paid actors—would have to be tapped into the same occult forces and be privy to the same demonic "enlightenment" as their predecessors at the Theosophical Society.).

A Return to Atlantis

At great sacrifice to themselves, we are told, the Hierarchy plans to some day enter again onto the physical plane of human affairs.

> Its appearance, expression and activity will be upon the physical plane for the first time since it withdrew into the subjective side of life and focused itself on the mental plane (instead of the physical) during the days of ancient Atlantis and after the war between the Lords of the Shining Countenance and Lords of the Dark Face, as *The Secret Doctrine* calls it.[23]

Atlantis was supposedly the most occult society ever to exist and was destroyed by the Great Flood. According to occult legend, Atlantis existed at the helm of a world government based on ten geopolitical regions and containing elements of democracy. However, because of the rampant and universal involvement of humans in the occult, demonic spirit beings had been invoked to the point where they were apparently enabled (or empowered) to physically manifest themselves and even to have sexual relations with women, producing a part human/ part supernatural offspring.

The Bible seems to support the fact that such beings dwelled for a time upon the earth. Genesis 6:4 (KJV) states:

> There were giants in the earth in those days; and also after that, when the sons of God came in unto the daughters of men, and they bare children to them, the same became mighty men which were of old, men of renown.

The Illustrated Bible's translation of the same passage is as follows:

> In those days, and even afterwards, when the evil beings from the spirit world were sexually involved with human women, their children became giants, of whom so many legends are told.

The New International Version refers to these "giants" or "sons of God" as the "Nephilim." *Unger's Bible Dictionary* offers the following explanation of "Nephilim":

> The Nephilim are considered by many as giant demigods, the unnatural offspring of the "daughters of men" (mortal women) in cohabitation with the "sons of God" (angels). This utterly unnatural union, violating God's created orders of being, was such a shocking

abnormality as to necessitate the worldwide judgment of the Flood.

The biblical reference here to "sons of God" clearly has a negative connotation and is actually referring to those angels which had rebelled against God. We know they were demonic beings, as their appearance is the last thing recorded in the Bible prior to God sending the Flood. God painfully realized that mankind had reached the point of no return. There had to be a new beginning to break man's infatuation with the occult and intermingling with these sexually perverted fallen angels (unclean spirits or demons).

Yet during our generation there has been an incredible resurgence of occult activity, and people are once again invoking "spirits" in massive numbers. These insights cause Jesus' words to take on a more literal meaning. Concerning the time immediately preceding His return to put an end to this evil, Jesus said: "As it was in the days of Noah, so it will be at the coming of the Son of Man" (Matt. 24:37, NIV).

In spite of all the clear warnings of Scripture, occult leaders are intent on returning the world to this "enlightened state." Masonic leaders of the past, such as Manly P. Hall and Albert Pike had much to say about Atlantis, the Flood, and the resurrection of occult activity after the Flood during the time of Nimrod and the Tower of Babel. Pike referred to Freemasonry as the "custodian" or special guardian of these occult secrets and revealed the hidden agenda of his institution—the forming of a Luciferic one-world government. (See pp. 121, 124, 144, and 145 of *En Route to Global Occupation.*) Alice Bailey, interestingly enough, like Blavatsky and Besant, was a well-known female Masonic leader of her day.

At the time this chapter was written, the featured movie on the local cable network was *Cocoon*. For months this movie was aired almost daily. Its occultic themes aren't difficult to spot even though they are presented through a well-directed, entertaining plot.

The main characters are originally from the legendary, sunken continent of Atlantis; they are beings of pure light; they have returned and they hold out the promise to humanity that if we will follow them, we won't ever die. "And the serpent said unto the woman, Ye shall not surely die" (Gen. 3:4). It would appear that at least one of the Masters of Wisdom has a "natural predisposition" to work in the entertainment field. Many movie themes today have an underlying New Age message. *Star Wars* teaches us about the "force," *E.T.* is a sweet little reptilian creature from another world, and *The Never Ending Story* teaches children that you can create your own reality.

The Work of the Hierarchy

A publication of Lucis Trust describes the progress of "the Hierarchy" very well.

> Hierarchical work is so quietly and smoothly developed and so effectively expressive of ex-

panding human consciousness, that when it is well advanced it appears quite natural and reasonable. In the early stages, however, it is generally considered radical and even revolutionary and often meets determined opposition ... The Masters work slowly and with deliberation, free from any sense of speed, toward their objective, but they do have a time limit ... There are periods of major opportunity of which the Hierarchy takes advantage and this present period is one of major opportunity.[24]

This time limit was foretold two thousand years ago when Jesus described the tribulation of the last days to the Apostle John. "And the great dragon was cast out, that old serpent, called the devil, and Satan, which deceiveth the whole world: he was cast out into the earth, and his angels were cast out with him.... Woe to the inhabiters of the earth and of the sea! For the devil is come down unto you, having great wrath, because he knoweth that he hath but a short time" (Rev. 12:9, 12b).

The Tibetan, Djwhal Khul tells us a little more about himself (or what he wants us to believe) in the book, *The Externalisation of the Hierarchy*.

Members of the Hierarchy do not as a rule intermingle largely with the public or walk the streets of our great cities. They work as I do from my retreat in the Himalayas, and from there I have influenced and helped far more people than I could possibly have reached had I walked daily in the midst of the noise and chaos of human affairs ... I reach

this vast number of human beings through
the books which I have written, through the
groups which I have started and impulsed,
such as World Goodwill and the Triangles,
and through my disciples who talk and spread
the truth as I have sought to present it.[25]

This demonic being states in another publication of Lucis Trust, "In 1919, during the month of November, I made contact with Alice Bailey and asked her to do some writing for me."[26] In her book *The Unfinished Autobiography*, her husband, Foster Bailey explains how this was done.

Mrs. Bailey gets in touch with the Tibetan . . .
he communicates with her telepathically. The
information is given with very great rapidity
and the detail teaching is impressed upon her
consciousness with such clarity that she is
enabled to write it down, so that no word is
changed.[27]

Many people have been intrigued by this form of writing. The psychologist, Carl Jung, whom we will study next, believed that The Tibetan was her personified higher self while Alice Bailey was her lower self. When the reality of Satan is denied, another explanation is always sought. The concept of the "higher self" is very popular today in explaining away demonic trance channeling.

Teachings of the Tibetan Master

There are four pillars upon which the New Age movement stands, and the writings of The

Tibetan through Alice Bailey reinforce all four. These pillars are evolution, reincarnation, astrology, and Eastern forms of meditation.

Evolution

In her *Unfinished Autobiography* Alice states, "All evolutionary development in all fields is an expression of divinity and the static condition of theological interpretation is contrary to the great law of the universe, evolution."[28]

Reincarnation

The entire concept of the Hierarchy is one of progress up the ladder of reincarnation until perfection is reached and one can move beyond the physical plane of existence. Of her own life, Alice states, "I know that I am today what many, many lives of experience and bitter lessons have made me."[29] Reincarnation is a substitute for the resurrection promised to all who belong to Christ.

Astrology

One of the twenty-four books written by The Tibetan is *A Treatise on the Seven Rays, Vol. III– Esoteric Astrology*. A few of the chapter titles in this work are: "The Zodiac and the Rays," "The Sacred and Non-Sacred Planets," and "The Nature of Esoteric Astrology." Seeking guidance through the stars and planets is Satan's substitute for the guidance of the Holy Spirit in a Christian's life.

Meditation

The Tibetan also had a great deal to say about meditation and placed great importance upon it. One of the books, which he wrote through Alice Bailey, was called *Letters on Occult Meditation*. Remember that all of this was written before 1949. Yet it seems that everything which was promoted in these books has completely permeated the culture of our day, in this country as well as throughout the rest of the world. In this book he states,

> One powerful stimulation to the mental rapport between East and West may be an increasing tendency for the Westerner to cultivate the science of meditation, long practiced in the East as an essential part of religious and spiritual experience. In this day and age, and as we enter into the mentally-oriented Age of Aquarius, with increasing numbers of men and women transferring from an emotional to a mental focus, the science of meditation as a mind training technique in concentration and invocation will become increasingly practiced in the West.[30]

They go on to predict that the growing influence of the "science" of meditation will eventually lead to the establishing of schools of meditation under the guidance and instruction of initiated disciples. Today these schools are flourishing in every major city in America. Transcendental meditation, forms of yoga and other "centering" techniques are now being taught to our children even in some public schools.

In the field of music, the latest trend is New Age meditative music, which is designed to put those who listen into an altered state of consciousness. Virtual reality is another new "technology" which attempts to fuse science with spiritual/occult phenomena, by automatically inducing an altered state of consciousness (or hypnotic trance) in individuals through some of the programs now available. It is being dubbed by some researchers as "the LSD of the nineties."

Organized Meditation

One of the organizations established by Alice Bailey to promote the "science of meditation" is called Triangles. A triangle is a group of three people who link each day in thought for a few minutes of "creative meditation." Many of these triangles involve people in more than one country. During the time of this "linkage," they believe that they are invoking the energies of light and goodwill. They visualize these energies as circulating through the three focal points of each triangle, and pouring out through the network of triangles surrounding the planet. At this time, they repeat the Great Invocation which we will discuss a little later.

In a paper put out by Lucis Trust, they make this statement about the concept of triangles,

> Men have the power, through focussed united invocation to affect world events. The massed thought power of men and women of goodwill can create a channel of communication

between God and man through which spiritual energies can flow to heal and rebuild a troubled world. It is this power, properly used and directed, that can be humanity's "saving force."[31]

As we will see in a later chapter dealing with the Planetary Commission, the plan of the Masters to involve the whole world in the belief of mind power through meditation has been abundantly fulfilled.

One of the techniques widely used in New Age groups and, more importantly, in many of our public schools today is that of focused or meditative visualization. Even in many of our churches, we are told that it is most important to visualize the answer to our prayers if we hope to get results. In other words, technique is everything! This is also the basis of most positive mental attitude seminars. The subtle message is that you can create your own reality through visualization. It would seem that we are right on target with the "Masters' Plan" when we look at what they said through Alice Bailey more than forty years ago. "The teaching on the New Discipleship includes the newer type of meditation emphasizing visualization and the use of creative imagination."[32]

The Bible tells us much about meditation, especially in the Psalms. We are to meditate (or reflect) upon God's Word, His goodness and mercy to us and the wonders of His creation. The biblical concept of meditation means "to think about or to dwell upon"; it involves an active thought process. This is far different from the Eastern forms of meditation that put the mind into a passive, neutral state, open to any forces that choose to enter. There is much beauty to behold in God's creation, but visualizing what isn't there won't bring it into being. It does, however, seem to open a door to demonic forces to work more effectively in our lives. The initial results may seem to get us what we desire, but the long-term results lead away from a biblical faith in God.

Divine Energy

Everywhere you turn in the New Age movement, one is confronted with terms such as "energy" and "vibrations." It would be well at this point to examine what is meant by these terms and to understand the concepts behind them. For the Christian, God is Sovereign Creator, Father and Redeemer. To the New Age mind, God is the sum of all creation, thus He is the energy that flows through all things. The Tibetan explains it very well.

> The esotericist of today is a practical worker. His illumined consciousness makes available to him a source of energy supply which is inexhaustible and which originates within the circulating energy of the One Life. He thus becomes a center of energy transmission between Hierarchy and humanity . . . Spiritual impression has been interrupted and there has been interference with the divine circulatory flow. It is the task of disciples of the world to restore this flow and to stop this interference.[33]

The interference probably comes from those "appalling, orthodox Fundamentalists" who never use their minds.

Lucis Trust, which was established in 1922 by Alice Bailey and her husband, Foster Bailey, exists to further the work that the Baileys were doing to promote the plan of the Hierarchy. Today it is still very much in operation and, until the mid-1980s, was directed by Mary Bailey, Foster's second wife. Their current address is at Cooper Station, New York, New York. They distribute volumes of material and run a flourishing correspondence school to educate disciples in the esoteric teachings of the Masters, including their ideas on meditation, energy, and how to invoke the appearance of "The Christ" and his accompanying New World Order.

The Great Invocation

The Great Invocation, given to Alice by The Tibetan as an invocatory prayer to the Hierarchy, is one of the most widely publicized activities of Lucis Trust. It has appeared as an advertisement in Reader's Digest and is included as a special insert in all of the Bailey books. The following is the most often used section of this invocation:

> From the point of Light within the Mind of God
> Let light stream forth into the minds of men.
> Let light descend on Earth.
>
> From the point of Love within the Heart of God
> Let love stream forth into the hearts of men.
> May Christ return to Earth.

> From the centre where the Will of God is known
> Let purpose guide the little wills of men—
> The purpose which the Masters know and serve.
>
> From the centre which we call the race of men
> Let the Plan of Love and Light work out
> And may it seal the door where evil dwells.
>
> Let Light and Love and Power restore the Plan on Earth.[34]

This well-publicized section was given to Alice in 1945. A lesser-known section, given in 1940, is most revealing. Part of this section states:

> Come forth, O Mighty One.
> The hour of service of the Saving Force has now arrived.
> Let it be spread abroad, O Mighty One.
>
> Let Light and Love and Power and Death
> Fulfill the purpose of the Coming One.[35]

The "Mighty One" or "the Christ" mentioned here by Bailey is in reality a reference to the future appearance of the anti-Christ (who some Bible scholars believe may actually come in the name of Christ—masquerading as the Messiah), an event described in 2 Thessalonians, chapter 2 as well as in Revelation, chapters 13 and 14, along with other passages of Scripture in the book of Daniel and 1 John. The anti-Christ, or Beast, will be Satan personified (in the flesh)— just as Jesus Christ was God manifested in the flesh. He will briefly rule the world during a period known in the Bible as "The Great Tribu-lation" (Rev. 7:14, also chapters 11-18), a three-

and-one-half year time span immediately preceding the true physical return, or second coming, of Jesus Christ at the end of this age. The
goal of this satanic being will be to gain the
worship and allegiance of man, an open and
rebellious defiance of God.

In another publication of Lucis Trust, in a
section entitled "Deeper Meaning of the Great
Invocation," disciples are told,

> The Great Invocation if given widespread dis-
> tribution, can be to the new world religion
> what the Lord's Prayer has been to Christian-
> ity. First, the general public will regard it as a
> prayer to God Transcendent. They will not
> recognize Him yet as imminent in His cre-
> ation. Secondly, esotericists, aspirants and
> spiritually-minded people will have a deeper
> and more understanding approach. To them
> it will convey the recognition of the world of
> causes and of Those Who stand subjectively
> behind world affairs, the spiritual Directors
> of our life . . . With this fundamental attitude,
> the necessity for a widespread expression of
> these underlying facts will be apparent and
> an era of spiritual propaganda, engineered
> by disciples and carried forward by esotericists,
> will mature.[36]

They tell us that when this plan is fulfilled,
it will strike a death blow to evil, selfishness and
separateness, sealing it into the tomb of death
forever. Of course separateness refers to those
who refuse to become a part of this new world
religion.

There is a message here for the Christian. If the forces of darkness place such importance on this invocation or prayer, there must be great spiritual power involved. Unfortunately, it is being utilized to call forth the forces of evil which are deceiving humanity today. How much more, then, should the Christian be praying to our heavenly Father, with whom all power resides. How many of us are so busy with "Christian service" that we never find time to enter into that most important time alone with God? The Scriptures tell us that we are in a spiritual battle and "the weapons of our warfare are not carnal, but mighty through God to the pulling down of strongholds" (2 Corinthians 10:4). The greatest of those weapons is the power of prayer.

The Role of the U.N.

As we have seen from the beginning, the ultimate goal of the New Age movement is a one world government, a one world economic system, and a one world religion, and all three are closely intertwined. Does Lucis Trust, a deceptive spiritual organization, have anything to say about a future government and economy? A booklet entitled *International Unity* from Lucis Trust gives us a clear picture of their position.

> It can be said that to the spiritual leaders of the race certain lines of action seem right and guarantee constructive attitudes. The United Nations, through the General Assembly, specialized agencies, and its various councils, commissions and committees must be supported; there is, as yet, no other organization

> to which man can hopefully look ... The
> world's economic councils must set the re-
> sources of the earth free for the use of
> humanity ... How can there be a fair distri-
> bution of the world's resources? How can true
> religion be resurrected and the ways of true
> spiritual living govern the hearts of men? ...
> Steadily and regularly the public should be
> taught an internationalism and a world unity
> which is based on simple goodwill and on
> cooperative interdependence.[37]

Obviously, control of the world's resources
is absolutely essential to the existence of a world
government, and control of the wealth of the
United States, which has been the result of the
free enterprise system, is one of the goals.

The next statements sound as if they had
been penned by "One Worlders" just last month,
but remember that the "Masters" have not spoken through Alice Bailey since her death in 1949.
It is obvious, however, that their work continues, and they are right on schedule.

> National selfishness and a fixed determina-
> tion to preserve national status must gradu-
> ally fade out ... The problem of the United
> Nations ... involves the right distribution of
> the world's resources ... The time will inevi-
> tably come when, in the interest of peace and
> security, the capitalists in the various nations
> will be forced to realize this and will also be
> forced to adopt the principle of sharing. The
> problem of distribution is not difficult once
> the food of the world is freed from politics
> and from capitalism.[38]

What they fail to mention is that no other nation on earth has so freely shared its wealth and resources with those in need in every part of the world. Is Russia the first to aid earthquake or flood victims? And do we regularly buy grain from Russian farmers because our free enterprise system has broken down so that we can't feed our own people? Let it also be remembered that by far the largest share of funding for relief agencies, like the International Red Cross, has come from the West. Along with this, hundreds of Christian ministries, which originate in the United States, have reached out to alleviate suffering in this world—more than any other private group of organizations in history. It is Christians such as Larry Jones of Feed the Children and others like him who are known for feeding and clothing the poor in other countries (with other systems of government and religion). It is not the Dalai Lama or the KGB. And what does Lucis Trust, itself, contribute to help the needy of the world, outside of their volumes of propaganda?

Yet Lucis Trust's propaganda tells us,

> The key to humanity's trouble, focussing as it has in the economic difficulties of the past two hundred years and in the theological impasse of the orthodox churches has been to take and not to give, to accept and not share, to grasp and not to distribute . . . These conditions are the result of religious faiths which have not moved forward in their thinking for hundreds of years . . . The powerful,

reactionary, conservative groups desirous of
retaining as much of the past as possible have
great power and no vision.[39]

The admiration and endorsement of the
United Nations by Lucis Trust is part of a "mu-
tual admiration society." Robert Muller, assistant secretary general of the United Nations from
1948 to 1984, is a devoted student of the works
of Alice Bailey. He has established a school for
the study of her teachings in Arlington, Texas.
The Robert Muller School, or the School of
Ageless Wisdom, as it is officially known, makes
this statement, "When some part of Universal
Truth has been truly grasped, the Source is
recognised to be beyond any scriptural authority."[40] They state that the school is not for the
beginner, but for the mentally developed, ma-
ture individual.

There is a well-known painting of Jesus standing outside the United Nations building in New
York City. He is seeking entrance but receives
no response and never will. This organization,
along with supporters like Lucis Trust, will bow
to no God except the divinity of man himself, as
taught by Lucifer. There can be no place for the
Prince of Peace in a world which is becoming
increasingly convinced that the old "Piscean Age"
and the "old forms of religion" are giving way
to the Age of Aquarius and the flowering of
human potential into a new golden era of peace
and brotherhood.

The Tibetan's Views on
Jews and Christians
(As channeled through Alice A. Bailey)

Alice A. Bailey and Lucis Trust have had a long history of promoting ideas that run contrary to the Bible and the historical teachings of Orthodox Christians and Jews. In fact, this is putting it mildly! Bailey's devious character is strongly reflected in her pronounced, but cleverly rationalized, anti-Jewish and anti-Christian statements, which permeate her writings.

She justifies the atrocities of the two world wars, including the Holocaust—in all its horror—as necessary developments in preparing the way for the coming New Age. Bailey also attempts to redefine the person of Jesus Christ and His teachings in order to fit her agenda. For example, she tries to explain away the atoning work of Jesus Christ on the cross and the fact that men are sinners in need of redemption, by stressing the divinity of man and the need for a new religion centered on this belief. What is further appalling is the way in which she refers to Jews and to true Christians and whatever is good according to biblical Christianity, as belonging to the Forces of Darkness. In short, she turns the truth upside down, calling good, evil, and evil, good.

The deceptive nature of her false teachings would be clear to any student who is firmly grounded in the Bible. However, her statements often contain certain grains of truth, which only

add to the subtlety of her message, thereby leading many astray. This is certainly typical of how
Satan operates. He usually masquerades as an
angel of light (2 Cor. 11:14), masterfully weav-
ing his web of deception around traces of truth
(twisting the truth). Jesus did not call him the
"father of lies" (John 8:44) for nothing.

Having warned the reader of Alice Bailey's
deceitful writings, I would like to close this chapter by allowing her words, as allegedly received
from the Tibetan Master, to speak for themselves. Although these teachings were supposedly not her own, she nevertheless accepted them
as her own beliefs.

Author's note: Many of the following quotes
contain references to "the Christ." These references, however, should not be understood to be
synonymous with Jesus Christ. Bailey considered
the title of Christ something that could be
earned. According to her beliefs, humans are
simply gods in the making; and we can all attain
the "Christ-consciousness." This belief is particularly appealing to pantheists. However, according to Bailey, "the Christ" also has a second,
more esoteric meaning, which she reveals on
page 558 of *The Externalisation of the Hierarchy*:

> The Tibetan has asked me [Alice Bailey] to
> make clear that when he is speaking of the
> Christ he is referring to His official name as
> Head of the Hierarchy. The Christ works for
> all men, irrespective of their faith; He does
> not belong to the Christian world any more
> than to the Buddhist, the Mohammedan or
> any other faith. There is no need for any man

> to join the Christian Church in order to be
> affiliated with Christ. The requirements are
> to love your fellowmen, lead a disciplined life,
> recognise the divinity in all faiths and all be-
> ings, and rule your daily life with Love. A.A.B.

I believe that Bailey's use of "the Christ" in
this context is simply a disguised reference to
what, according to Scripture, would be termed
"the anti-Christ" (1 John 2:18). It is a further
example of how Bailey and the Tibetan have
inverted the truth.

The Jews Are the Problem

"I am considering the world problem, centering around the Jews as a whole" (*The
Externalisation of the Hierarchy* [January 1939], p.
74).

> The Jew, with his emphasis upon his position
> as one of the 'chosen people,' has stood sym-
> bolically throughout the centuries as the rep-
> resentative of the wandering, incarnating soul,
> but the Jewish people have never recognised
> the symbolic mission with which their race
> was entrusted, and they have taken to them-
> selves the glory and the honour of the Lord's
> elect. The Jew made this mistake and, as an
> Oriental race, the Jews have failed to hold
> before the Orient the divine nature of man-
> kind as a whole, for all are equally divine and
> all are the Lord's elect. (*The Destiny of the
> Nations* [1939], pp. 34–35)

> It may interest you to know that the Christ
> has not yet decided what type of physical ve-
> hicle He will employ should He take physical

form and work definitely upon the physical
plane. He waits to see what nation or group
of nations do the most work in preparation
for His reappearance. He will *not*, however,
take a Jewish body as He did before, for the
Jews have forfeited that Privilege. The Messiah for Whom they wait will be one of Christ's
senior disciples, but it will *not* be, as originally
intended, the Christ. Symbolically, the Jews
represent (from the point of view of the Hierarchy) that from which all Masters of the
Wisdom and Lords of Compassion emerge:
materialism, cruelty and a spiritual conserva-
tism, so that today they live in *Old Testament*
times and are under the domination of the
separative, selfish, lower concrete mind.

But their opportunity will come again, and
they may change all this when the fires of
suffering at last succeed in purifying them
and burning away their ancient crystallisation,
thus liberating them to the extent that they
can recognise their Messiah, Who will *not*,
however, be the world Messiah. The Jews need
humility more than any other nation. By humility they may learn something of value. (*The
Rays and the Initiations*, 1st ed. [1960], pp.
705–706)

There are certain areas of evil in the world
today through which these forces of darkness
can reach humanity. What they are and where
they are I do not intend to say. I would point
out, however, that Palestine should no longer
be called the Holy Land; its sacred places are
only the passing relics of three dead and gone
religions. The spirit has gone out of the old
faiths and the true spiritual light is transfer-

ring itself into a new form which will manifest on earth eventually as the new world religion. . . .

Judaism is old, obsolete and separative and has no true message for the spiritually-minded which cannot be better given by the newer faiths. . . .

the Christian faith also has served its purpose; its Founder seeks to bring a new Gospel and a new message that will enlighten all men everywhere. Therefore, Jerusalem stands for nothing of importance today, except for that which has passed away and should pass away. The "Holy Land" is no longer holy, but is desecrated by selfish interests, and by a basically separative and conquering nation. (*The Rays and the Initiations* [1943-1947], p. 754)

The World Tension Analysed

The tension in the world today, particularly in the Hierarchy, is such that it will produce another and perhaps ultimate world crisis, or else such a speeding up of the spiritual life of the planet that the coming in of the long-looked-for New Age conditions will be amazingly hastened. . . .

The area of difficulty—as is well known—is the Near East and Palestine. The Jews, by their illegal and terroristic activities, have laid a foundation of great difficulty for those who are seeking to promote world peace . . . the Jews have partially again opened the door to the Forces of Evil . . . Palestine is no longer a Holy Land and should not be so regarded. . . .

It is the Zionists who have defied the United Nations, lowered its prestige and made its position both negative and negligible to the world. It is the Zionists who have perpetrated the major act of aggression since the formation of the United Nations, and who were clever enough to gain the endorsement of the United Nations, turning the original 'recommendation' of the United Nations into an order. The rule of force, of aggression and of territorial conquest by force of arms is demonstrated today by the Zionists in Palestine, as well as the demonstration of the power of money to purchase governments. These activities run counter to all the plans of the spiritual Hierarchy and make a point of triumph of the forces of evil. (*The Rays and the Initiations* [April 1947], pp. 428–430 and 634–636)

The Forces of Darkness are powerful energies, working to preserve that which is ancient and material . . . they work to prevent the understanding of that which is of the New Age; they endeavor to preserve that which is familiar and old, to counteract the effects of the oncoming culture and civilisation, to bring blindness to the peoples and feed steadily the existing fires of hate, of separateness, of criticism and of cruelty. . . .

Our earth humanity and the group of human beings who are far more ancient in their origin than we are, will form one humanity and then there will be peace on earth. . . .

The solution will come . . . when the races regard the Jewish problem as a humanitarian problem. . . . He [the Jew] must let go of his own separative tendencies and of his deep sense of persecution. [Remember this was written January 1939.] He will do this latter with great facility, when he grasps, as a race, the significance and inevitability of the Law of Karma, and . . . realises that the law is working out and incidentally releasing him for a greater future. (*The Externalisation of the Hierarchy* [January 1939], pp. 75–78)

"The War" Was Good!
The Death and Destruction Was Necessary

The great energy of purification [Shamballa forces] is regenerating humanity, and of this the wide spread fires which have been such an outstanding characteristic of this war (1914-1945) are the outward and visible sign. Much evil is being burnt out through the revelation of the appalling character of that evil, and through this, unity is being produced . . . The energy of destruction has its side of beauty when the spiritual values are grasped. (*The Rays and the Initiations* [April 1943], p. 86, ref. p. 76)

This world crisis, with all its horror and suffering, is—in the last analysis—the result of successful evolutionary processes. . . .

Today we are watching the death of a civilisation or cycle of incarnation of humanity. . . . worn out religious dogmas and the grip of theology and the orthodox churches have no longer sufficed to hold the allegiance of the potent, inner, spiritual life. . . . There is everywhere a cry for change and for those new forms in the religious, political, educational and economic life of the race which will allow . . . better spiritual expression. Such a change is rapidly coming and is regarded by some as death—terrible and to be avoided if possible. It is indeed death but it is beneficent and needed. . . .

That humanity is bringing about this needed change in unnecessary, cruel and painful ways is indeed true . . . Nevertheless, for the progress of the soul . . . death is inevitable, good and necessary . . . But we need to remember that the worst death of all . . . would be if a form of civilisation or a body form became static and eternal; if the old order never altered and the old values were never transmuted into higher and better ones, that would indeed be a disaster. . . .

This stage of death and of birth . . . can be easily grasped by the esotericist as he studies the world war in its two distinctive periods: 1914 to 1918, and 1939 until 1942. The first stage . . . was most definitely the death stage; the second stage, in which we now find ourselves, is literally the stage of birth—the birth pangs of the new order and of the new civilisation. . . .

Such a dying is ever a painful process. Pain has always been the purifying agent, employed by the Lords of Destiny, to bring about liberation. The accumulated pain of the present war and the inherited pain of the earlier stage (begun in 1914) is bringing about a salutary and changing world consciousness. The Lord of Pain has descended from His throne and is treading the ways of earth today, bringing distress, agony and terror to those who cannot interpret His ends. (*The Externalisation of the Hierarchy* [September 1939], pp. 113–116)

Others again may have faint glimmerings of this new approach to God and service, which—again I say—can and must remake, rebuild, and rehabilitate the world. . . . Those who seek to evoke the Shamballa force, are approaching close to the energy of fire. . . . Fire was an outstanding aspect of the war. . . . This was the great menacing and chosen means of destruction in this war. This is a fulfillment of the ancient prophecy, that the attempt to destroy the Aryan race will be by means of fire, just as ancient Atlantis was destroyed by water. But, fiery good will and the conscious focussed use of the Shamballa force, can counter fire by fire, and this must be done. (*Esoteric Astrology*, 1st ed. [1951], pp. 586–587)

To many of you . . . the World War was a supreme disaster, an agony to be averted in the future at any cost, a dire and dreadful happening indicative of the wickedness of man and the incredible blind indifference of God. To us, on the inner side, the World War was in the nature of a major surgical operation made in an effort to save the patient's life. A violent streptococcic germ and infection had menaced the life of humanity (speaking in symbols) and an operation was made in order to prolong opportunity and save life, *not* to save the form. This operation was largely successful. The germ, to be sure, is not eradicated and makes its presence felt in infected areas in the body of humanity.

Another surgical operation may be necessary, not in order to destroy and end the present civilisation, but in order to dissipate the infection and get rid of the fever. It may not, however, be needed, for a process of dissipation, distribution and absorption has been going on and may prove effective. Let us work towards that end. But at the same time, let us never forget that it is the *Life*, its purpose and its directed intentional destiny that is of importance; and also that when a form proves inadequate, or too diseased, or too crippled for the expression of that purpose, it is—from the point of view of the Hierarchy—no disaster when that form has to go. Death is not a disaster to be feared; the work of the Destroyer is not really cruel or undesirable. (*Education in the New Age*, 1st ed. [1954], pp. 111–112)

The Planned Destruction of Western Civilization
(Judeo-Christian Culture)

The Hierarchy is deeply concerned over world events. . . . The New Age is upon us and we are witnessing the birth pangs of the new culture and the new civilisation. This is now in progress. That which is old and undesirable must go and of these undesirable things, hatred and the spirit of separation must be the first to go. (*The Externalisation of the Hierarchy* [25 September 1938], pp. 61–62)

The Hierarchy is struggling hard with the so-called "forces of evil," and the New Group of World Servers is the instrument. . . .

The forces of evil are ... the entrenched ancient ideals ... which must now disappear if the New Age is to be ushered in as desired. The old established rhythms, inherent in the old forms of religion, of politics and of the social order, must give place to newer ideals, to the synthetic understanding, and to the new order. The laws and modes of procedure which are characteristic of the New Age must supersede the old, and these will, in time, institute the new social order and the more inclusive regime. (*Esoteric Psychology II*, 1st ed. [1942] pp. 630–631)

They [France, Germany, Italy, Spain and Portugal] have ... reacted to that force [Shamballa Force] through the medium of certain great and outstanding personalities who were peculiarly sensitive to the will-to-power and the will-to-change and who ... have altered the character of their national life, and emphasised increasingly the wider human values. The men who inspired the initiating French revolution; the great conqueror, Napoleon; Bismarck, the creator of a nation; Mussolini, the regenerator of his people; Hitler who lifted a distressed people upon his shoulders; Lenin, the idealist; Stalin and Franco are all expressions of the Shamballa force and of certain little understood energies. These have wrought significant changes in their day and generation. ...

We call these people dictators, demagogues, inspired leaders, or just and wise men, according to our peculiar ideology, tradition, attitudes to our fellowmen and our particular political, economic and religious training. But all these leaders are ... in the last analysis, highly developed personalities. They are being used to engineer great and needed changes and to alter the face of civilisation. . . .

Blame not the personalities involved or the men who produce these events before which we stand today bewildered and appalled. They are only the product of the past and the victims of the present. At the same time, they are the agents of destiny, the creators of the new order and the initiators of the new civilisation; they are the destroyers of what must be destroyed before humanity can go forward along the Lighted Way. (*The Externalisation of the Hierarchy* [1939], pp. 133–135)

I write for the generation which will come ... at the end of this century; they will inaugurate the framework, structure and fabric of the New Age ... which will develop the civilisation of the Aquarian Age. This coming age will be as predominantly the age of group interplay, group idealism and group consciousness as the Piscean Age has been one of personality unfoldment ... for the will of the individual will voluntarily be blended into group will. (*The Rays and the Initiations* [1943-1947], p. 109)

It will be for humanity then to precipitate and stabilise the appearing good, and this they will learn to do through the utilisation of the third Shamballa energy—the energy of organisation. The new world will be built upon the ruins of the old. The new structure will rise. (*The Rays and the Initiations* [1943-1947], p. 88)

Christianity to Be Conquered or Redefined

I refer to that period which will surely come in which an *Enlightened People* will rule; these people will not tolerate authoritarianism in any church . . . they will not accept or permit the rule of any body of men who undertake to tell them what they must believe in order to be saved . . . (*The Reappearance of the Christ* 1st ed. [1948], pp. 164–165)

World unity will be a fact when the children of the world are taught that religious differences are largely a matter of birth; that if a man is born in Italy, the probability is that he will be a Roman Catholic; if he is born a Jew, he will follow the Jewish teaching; if born in Asia, he may be a Mohammedan, a Buddhist, or belong to one of the Hindu sects; if born in other countries, he may be a Protestant and so on. He will learn that the religious differences are largely the result of man made quarrels over human interpretations of truth. Thus gradually, our quarrels and differences will be offset and the idea of the One Humanity will take their place. (*Education in the New Age* 1st ed. [1954], p. 88)

Recognition of the successful work of the New Group of World Servers will be accorded by the Hierarchy, and the testimony of the recognition will be the appearing of a symbol in the aura of . . . the entire group. This will be a symbol projected by the Hierarchy, specifically by the Christ . . . It is "the mark of a Saviour" and it will embody the mark or indication (the signature as medieval occultists

used to call it) of a new type of salvation or
salvage. Up till now the mark of the Saviour
has been the Cross, and the quality of the
salvation offered has been freedom from sub-
stance or the lure of matter and from its hold—
a freedom only to be achieved at a great cost.
The future holds within its silence other modes
of saving humanity. The cup of sorrow and
the agony of the Cross are well-nigh finished.
Joy and strength will take their place. Instead
of sorrow we shall have a joy which will work
out in happiness and lead eventually to bliss.
(*The Rays and the Initiations*, 1st ed. [1957],
pp. 233-234)

There is, as you well know, no angry God, no
hell, and no vicarious atonement . . . and the
only hell is the earth itself, where we learn to
work out our own salvation . . . This teaching
anent hell is a remainder of the sadistic turn
which was given to the thinking of the Christian Church in the Middle Ages and to the
erroneous teaching to be found in the Old
Testament anent Jehovah, the tribal God of
the Jews. Jehovah is *not* God . . . As these erroneous ideas die out, the concept of hell will
fade from man's recollection and its place
will be taken by an understanding of the law
which makes each man work out his own
salvation . . . which leads him to right the
wrongs which he may have perpetuated in his
lives on Earth, and which enables him eventually to "clean his own slate." (*Esoteric Healing*,
1st ed. [1953], p. 393)

The failure of Christianity can be traced to its
Jewish background (emphasised by St. Paul),
which made it full of propaganda instead of

loving action, which taught the blood sacrifice instead of loving service, and which emphasised the existence of a wrathful God, needing to be placated by death, and which embodied the threats of the Old Testament Jehovah in the Christian teaching of hell fire.

This situation is one which the Christ is seeking to alter; it has been in preparation for His instituting a new and more correct presentation of divine truth that I have sought—with love and understanding—to point out the faults of the world religions, with their obsolete theologies and their lack of love, and to indicate the evils of Judaism. The present world faiths must return to their early simplicity, and orthodox Judaism, with its deep-seated hate, must slowly disappear; all must be changed in preparation for the revelation which Christ will bring. (*The Externalisation of the Hierarchy*, 1st ed. [1957], pp. 542–543)

It can be expected that the orthodox Christian will at first reject the theories about the Christ which occultism presents; at the same time, this same orthodox Christian will find it increasingly difficult to induce the intelligent masses of people to accept the impossible Deity and the feeble Christ, which historical Christianity has endorsed. A Christ Who is present and living, Who is known to those who follow Him, Who is a strong and able executive and not a sweet and sentimental sufferer, Who has never left us but Who has worked for two thousand years through the medium of His disciples, the inspired men and women of all faiths . . . Who has no use for fanaticism or hysterical devotion but Who loves all men persistently, intelligently and optimistically, Who sees divinity in them all and Who comprehends the techniques of the evolutionary development of the human consciousness . . . these ideas the intelligent public can and will accept. (*The Externalisation of the Hierarchy*, 1st ed. [1957], pp. 589–590)

A Final Comment

I would like to take this opportunity to strongly urge every person reading this book to do whatever is possible to take a stand against the dangerous false teachings of the occult, such as those presented by Alice Bailey and Lucis Trust. Exposing anti-Semitic and anti-Christian teachings and actions should be a regular part of every Christian believer's life. It is because so few people speak out to warn others, that the enemy is able to make the alarming progress he is making in these days. We should all be disturbed by the fact that many of the preceding views have gained widespread acceptance, even in some Christian circles.

Jesus warned us that times such as these would come immediately prior to His return:

> As Jesus was sitting on the Mount of Olives, the disciples came to him privately. "Tell us," they said, "when will this happen and what will be the sign of your coming and of the end of the age?"

> Jesus answered: "Watch out that no one deceives you. For many will come in my name, claiming, 'I am the Christ,' and will deceive many . . ."

> "At that time many will turn away from the faith and will betray and hate each other, and many false prophets will appear and deceive many people . . ."

> "At that time if anyone says to you, 'Look, here is the Christ!' or, 'There he is!' do not believe it. For false Christs and false prophets will appear and perform great signs and miracles to deceive even the elect—if that were possible. See, I have told you ahead of time." (Matt. 24:3-5, 10-11, 23-25 [NIV])

Just because these things were prophesied to occur, however, does not mean we should sit back and do nothing to stand in their way. To the contrary, we must expose the works of darkness while sharing the hope we have in Jesus Christ with everyone who is willing to listen, even if this constitutes only a minority of the world's people.

The fact that Jesus prophesied these events would take place means only that He knew these evil times would eventually come. It does not mean that He condones this evil, nor does it mean that He wants His people to help bring evil about by doing nothing to stand in its way. Ephesians 5:11 (NIV) states, "Have nothing to do with the fruitless deeds of darkness, but rather expose them."

The day may soon come when Christians will be required to lay down their lives because of their beliefs. But, regardless of this, we must continue to raise a standard so that the world will be without excuse for its defiant ways, and in order that the truth of Jesus Christ may be proclaimed.

> Therefore put on the full armor of God, so
> that when the day of evil comes, you may be
> able to stand your ground, and after you have
> done everything, to stand. (Eph. 6:13 [NIV])

Chapter Two

◇

Presenting the Occult as a Science

Where is the wise man? Where is the scholar? Where is the philosopher of this age? Has not God made foolish the wisdom of the world?
—1 Corinthians 1:20 (NIV)

See to it that no one takes you captive through hollow and deceptive philosophy, which depends on human tradition and the basic principles of this world rather than on Christ.
—Colossians 2:8 (NIV)

Helena Blavatsky and Alice Bailey both lived in the world of the occult, and although their writings have the appearance of scholarly endeavors and have been accepted by some of the world's most powerful elite, their followers were generally not from among the highly educated in the intellectual community. However, while these first foundation stones were being put in

place, the groundwork was also being laid in the
academic world. The next two people we want
to study were scholars who not only believed
themselves to be theologians of sorts, but were
also involved in the sciences. The followers of
Carl Jung and Pierre Teilhard de Chardin come
from among the educated. Their disciples are
among the most highly respected in the fields
of psychology and philosophy and in the liberal
"academic" churches who preach merely a social gospel and "liberation theology."

In the *Aquarian Conspiracy*, a best-selling book
endorsing the New Age movement, author
Marilyn Ferguson took a survey of the practices
and beliefs of leading New Agers. When asked
to name individuals whose ideas had influenced
them the most, either through personal contact
or through their writings, the two most often
named were Carl Jung and Pierre Teilhard de
Chardin.[1] She also noted that 81 percent of those
responding were no longer active in the religion
of their childhood. It is interesting to note that
this is also true for three of the four people we
are studying in these first two chapters. In the
case of the fourth, his writings were banned by
his own church.

Carl Gustav Jung

Carl Jung was born on 26 July 1875 in
Kesswil, a small village on Lake Constance in
Switzerland, the same year that Helena Blavatsky
started the Theosophical Society. As is so often
the case, when Satan finds a likely channel to

use for furthering his web of deception, one can usually find evidence of occultic activities in that person's family background. Carl Jung was no exception.

Jung, himself, reported that his maternal grandfather, who was the vicar of Kesswil, was said to have "second sight" and carried on lively conversations with the dead. He always believed himself to be surrounded by ghosts. "My mother often told me how she had to sit behind him while he wrote his sermons, because he could not bear to have ghosts pass behind him while he was studying. The presence of a living being at his back frightened them away."[2]

It seems that this inclination was passed on to his mother. In his autobiography, *Memories, Dreams, Reflections*, he relates that at night the atmosphere in his parents' house would begin to thicken.

> From the door to my mother's room came a frightening influence. At night Mother was strange and mysterious. One night I saw coming from her door a faintly luminous indefinite figure whose head detached itself from the neck and floated along in front of it, in the air like a little moon.[3]

In spite of all this, or maybe because of it, Jung felt close to his mother. He felt that she was rooted in deep invisible ground that had nothing to do with the Christian faith. That ground seemed more connected to the things of nature such as animals, trees, meadows and running waters. He felt a close affinity for all of this in his own life and admitted that he never realized how pagan this foundation was. He would spend many hours sitting on a large rock behind their house, and at times would have trouble distinguishing if he was the boy sitting on the rock or the rock being sat upon by the boy. In short, he felt a oneness with nature.

Once his mother read to him from a richly illustrated children's book which contained an account of exotic religions, especially that of the Hindus. There were illustrations of Brahma, Vishnu and Shiva which were for him an inexhaustible source of interest. He would return to these pictures over and over.

His understanding of Jesus became distorted at an early age. He associated Jesus with death and the men in black coats and top hats that put people in a box in the ground. He was told by his preacher-father that Lord Jesus had taken them unto Himself. He also associated Jesus with a Jesuit priest that had frightened him once and, more importantly, with a strange dream that had a great influence on his life. It was a frightening dream of an underground temple and throne room and other erotic symbolism.

In his autobiography, he relates the importance of this dream.

> Through this childhood dream I was initiated into the secrets of the earth. What happened then was a kind of burial in the earth, and many years were to pass before I came out again. Today I know that it happened in order to bring the greatest possible amount of light into the darkness. It was an initiation

into the realm of darkness. My intellectual
life had its unconscious beginnings at that
time.[4]

Rejection of Christianity

Jung rejected the established doctrines of
Christianity for a religion based upon experience. He often stated that he doesn't believe, he
only knows, based upon his own experience. He
gained this experience from a life lived in the
internal regions of his own "psyche." His internal world of dreams and visions was always more
real to him than the external world of objective
reality. He rejected the religion of his father,
whom he considered to be a weak and tragic
failure who preached a shallow message of the
love and grace of God. Carl's god, on the other
hand, represented a cataclysmic shift from one
of dogma to one of myth, from Christianity to
psychology and from the conscious to the unconscious.

First Corinthians, chapter three, verse eleven
says, "For other foundation can no man lay than
that is laid, which is Jesus Christ." Carl Jung
built upon a faulty foundation from the beginning. The tragedy today is to see the thousands
of people who study his teachings with almost a
religious fervor and reverence. In every major
city of our country there are Friends of Jung
study groups, going by that name or some other,
and Jungian analysts can be visited to help one
"explore your inner depths."

The New Age movement of today is one that
bases its spiritual truth upon personal experi-

ence and not upon established fact and biblical truth. That experience is gained from going within. Carl Jung, more than anyone else, created the atmosphere for this concept to flourish. In a nearby city, the local Jungian analyst at one time was a pastor in a local Christian church. Now, after studying for five years at the Carl Jung Institute in Zurich, which one biographer refers to as "the mystical body of Carl Jung," he has abandoned his own foundation to join Jung in the subjective world within.

In spite of all the New Age talk about helping humanity and creating a better world, it is the followers of Jesus Christ—composing the Christian church and its many ministries—that have done more to alleviate human suffering than any other people in the world. Jesus spent his days involved with people, and He ministered to their needs to the point of personal exhaustion. And even though He was the one man who was truly divine, during his long nighttime vigils, He prayed to His Father in heaven, not to His "Higher Self" or to the "God within."

Jung himself said that he experienced an initiation into the realm of darkness. In the Gospel of John, we are told of Jesus,

> In him was life; and the life was the light of men. And the light shineth in darkness; and the darkness comprehended it not. . . . And this is the condemnation, that light is come into the world, and men loved darkness rather than light, because their deeds were evil. (John 1:4-5, 3:19)

It is worth noting that there are at least twelve references to Carl Jung and his concepts in Nevill Drury's *Dictionary of Mysticism and the Occult*. On page 137 of that dictionary, Drury states,

> In his later years, Jung became absorbed with ancient cosmologies and spent a considerable time analyzing Gnostic, alchemical, and mystical systems of thought. He provided commentaries for Richard Wilhelm's translations of the *I Ching*.[5]

Jung's Personal Theology

For a period of about six years, Jung worked closely with Sigmund Freud. Although Freud is better known among the general public, it is Carl Jung who has had the most influence on intellectuals leaning toward mystical New Age concepts. His ideas and teachings on the collective unconscious, the archetypes and their symbolism paved a broad path to lead people away from the beauty and simplicity of God's created order.

The Jungian concept of the collective unconscious holds that each individual is an island, joined together by a sort of underwater continent of unconscious thought. Picture a hand with the tips of the fingers above water, conversing and interacting with each other. Yet under the surface of the water, they are really connected to the palm of the hand and thus to each other. Each person, Jung believed, has those personal forgotten thoughts and experiences, but there is a collective unconscious mind of the entire race. Jung sometimes referred to the collective unconscious as the "psychic residue of human evolutionary development."

For Jung, the archetypes lie within the collective unconscious. An archetype, according to Jung, is a universal thought form or predisposition to perceive the world in certain ways. These archetypes appear to us in personified or symbolized pictorial form through dreams, myths, art and ritual. He believed that they represented the total latent potentiality of the psyche. So when we get in touch with them, we go beyond developing our individual potentialities and become incorporated in the eternal cosmic process. Some of Jung's archetypes are birth, death, magic, the hero, God, the demon and the earth mother. In the process of Jung's psychology, God is reduced to an archetype, a type of universal myth.

This is explained in a popular college textbook on psychology called *Personality Theories: An Introduction.*

> Whether or not God exists is not a question that Jung tried to answer. That which has no effect on us might as well not exist. Analytical psychology posits the existence of the archetypal God image—not God. Insofar as the archetype of God has a demonstrably clear effect on us, God is a psychic fact and a useful concept in our psychology. . . . Even more, attuning oneself to one's unconscious forces is a religious experience entailing acceptance of God. To be sure, the God that is accepted may not be the traditional deity of theism;

rather, it is an indwelling god, a natural spirit within the universal psyche of man.[6]

Is it any wonder that so many of our sons and daughters, who go off to the college campus, find their faith challenged and often shattered by this pseudoacademic atmosphere; when in reality modern psychology, presented as a science, is a bankrupt "religion" with no real capacity for helping people? Under the guise of psychology, spiritual/occultic concepts have gained acceptance as being legitimate scientific principles. Hence, occultism is increasingly going forth in the name of psychology and the "human sciences."

This textbook goes on to say,

> Jung's ideas have appealed to those who are discontent with Western society and its modes of exploration and who seek to expand their self-understanding by studying Eastern thought with its emphasis on introspection and experience . . . His concept of God as revealing himself through the collective unconscious is particularly attractive to theologians who seek a more relevant articulation of traditional theistic concepts . . . Jung's thinking compliments the recent interest in the East.[7]

Carl Jung also believed that dreams were of great significance and based much of his teaching on the interpretation of his own dreams. Today Jungian analysts train their students to keep dream journals and seek guidance for their lives from those dreams. God can certainly speak through dreams as He did when He told Joseph to take Mary as his wife. However, to believe that every dream is a form of guidance for one's life is to stand on shaky ground indeed.

Listen to the words of the prophet Jeremiah concerning false prophets and the relating of dreams.

> I have heard what the prophets said, that prophesy lies in my name, saying, I have dreamed, I have dreamed! . . . The prophet that hath a dream, let him tell a dream; and he that hath my word, let him speak my word faithfully. What is the chaff to the wheat? saith the Lord. . . . Behold, I am against them that prophesy false dreams, saith the Lord, and do tell them, and cause my people to err by their lies, and by their lightness; yet I sent them not, nor commanded them: therefore they shall not profit this people at all, saith the Lord. (Jer. 23:25, 28, 32)

A friend of mine once sat in the sanctuary of a local Christian church that displays a beautiful banner which says, Worthy is the Lamb, and yet simultaneously heard the occult glorified, ESP explained in a favorable light and demon possession passed off as only another form of guidance—in reference to someone's mind being taken over by an alien being. All of this was done by a specialist in Jungian psychology who was flown in from across the country for a special weekend seminar, with the full approval of the pastor.

Was Carl Jung a false prophet and are his followers being led astray into New Age think-

ing by following his teachings? I rest my case
with the words of Jeremiah,

> For both prophet and priest are profane; yea,
> in my house have I found their wickedness,
> saith the Lord. . . . I have not sent these proph-
> ets, yet they ran: I have not spoken to them,
> yet they prophesied. But if they had stood in
> my counsel, and had caused my people to
> hear my words, then they should have turned
> them from their evil way, and from the evil of
> their doings. (Jer. 23:11, 21-22)

Pierre Teilhard de Chardin

In studying the writings of a wide variety of
New Age political and spiritual leaders, one name
is praised over and over again. That name is
Pierre Teilhard de Chardin. His concepts and
teachings run like a continuous thread through
an intricate tapestry of today's New Age spiritual beliefs. Everywhere I turn, I see the imprint
of his thinking on the minds of individuals who
have rejected the God of the Bible for a god
who is nothing more than the "energy" that flows
through the sum of all creation. The circle of
Chardin's influence continues to widen, even
after his death, for not only did he write a number of widely read volumes, but many of his
disciples have their works on the best-seller lists.

An Obsession with Evolution

Pierre Teilhard de Chardin was born on 1
May 1881 in Sarcenat, France. He came from a
traditional Catholic family, the fourth of eleven
children. His father, Emmanuel, took pleasure

in teaching his children how to understand and appreciate natural history. So it is easy to understand how Teilhard became interested in the study of geology at an early age.

While there is nothing wrong with the study of geology for the purpose of exploring and developing natural resources such as oil and coal, for example, most writers of geology textbooks seem to be intent on promoting the theory of evolution. As one who studied geology in high school, I can personally attest to this fact. There has been no more successful strategy of Satan in preparing our world for the last great delusion than establishing in the minds of men the concept of evolution. This concept became the passion of Teilhard's life and every other pursuit; especially Christianity was forced to conform and subjugate itself to this supreme belief. He became a Jesuit priest, but instead of shepherding a parish or following some other religious work, he always pursued his first love, which was the blending of the physical and spiritual worlds under the banner of evolution.

Teilhard was a pantheist, despite his protests to the contrary. A pantheist is one who sees the universe as the one and only reality and calls this "God." Individual human beings are only phases or sparks of that greater reality. According to this theology, the earth itself, as well as man, is divine. Many of Teilhard's statements reflect this view of existence. He speaks about loving, adoring and serving the earth in the same way many Christians would speak about loving

God. He once said, "I want to love Christ with all my strength in the very act of loving the universe . . . Besides communion with the earth, is there not also communion with God in and through the earth?"[8]

Unfortunately, the Christ which Teilhard loved is not the Christ of the Gospels, but one of his own making. For him, Christ had to fit into his theory of evolution. He attempted to "pan-christify" the universe (turn it into Christ) and stated that Christ and the universe formed a mysterious compound which he named the Christ-Universal. For Teilhard, Christ was the "true soul of the World," the world representing his body or flesh. In *The Future of Man* he says,

> We cannot continue to love Christ without discovering Him more and more. The maturing of a collective consciousness accompanied by numerical expansions: these are two aspects inseparably linked to the historical unfolding of the Incarnation . . . Without the process of biological evolution, which produced the human brain, there would be no sanctified souls; and similarly, without the evolution of collective thought, through which alone the plenitude of human consciousness can be attained on earth, how can there be a consummated Christ?[9]

According to Teilhard's concept of evolution, at one time God was not highly evolved enough to express himself through human consciousness. This was during the prehistoric period when God could only express himself through animals. So in other words, evolution is simply man (and God) becoming conscious of himself; and Christ, in this scheme, is incarnate in the entire universe. Christ in his cosmic or universal nature overshadows Christ in his human nature.

> Christ is above all "the God of Evolution." He is its center, its Alpha and Omega, beginning and end. He is the Omega Point, the supreme summit of the evolutionary movement in which he is immersed and which super-animates. As "God the Evolver," he is the director, the leader, the cause and mover of evolution. Christ also is evolving into a Super-Christ. Humanity is the highest phase so far of evolution, but evolution is beginning to change into a Super-Humanity, which at its peak becomes the Omega Point.[10]

Teilhard de Chardin's theology diverged so far from biblical teaching that in 1957 the Catholic Holy Office decreed that his works must be withdrawn from libraries, seminaries and religious institutions. In 1962, the office issued a further warning to bishops, rectors of seminaries and presidents of universities to protect the minds of the faithful against the heresies of Chardin's teachings. However, this did not put an end to the influence of this French priest-paleontologist-philosopher. Today, he is praised in progressive Catholic circles as a great religious thinker and a scientific genius.

His influence goes far beyond Catholic circles as evidenced by the fact that he is the most widely read author in the New Age movement. In my local New Age, occultic bookstore, there is a display of bookmarks near the cash register with about ten famous (in their estimation) people pictured on them. Chardin is one of them. In the *Aquarian Conspiracy*, arguably the most important and comprehensive modern work on the New Age movement (by a New Ager), there are at least sixteen different references to Pierre Teilhard de Chardin.

A Political Influence

Former Democratic governor of New York, Mario Cuomo, who finished first in his class in law school, reads Teilhard de Chardin's works and gives copies of his books as gifts to interested friends. Cuomo was at one time considered to be a leading contender for the U.S. presidency.

Trilateralist, Zbigniew Brzezinski appears to be another follower of Chardin. On page 73 of his book, *Between Two Ages*, he quotes Chardin as saying, "Monstrous as it is, is not modern totalitarianism really the distortion of something magnificent, and thus quite near to the truth?"[11]

Robert Muller, the lawyer-economist, began his work at the United Nations in 1948 and was assistant secretary general until 1984. It was through his associations in that institution that he too became a follower of Chardin. In his book, *New Genesis–Shaping a Global Spirituality*, he tells of his spiritual growth in a chapter entitled, "My Five Teilhardian Enlightenments." It was originally U Thant, a Buddhist (and former U.N. secretary general), who kept telling Muller about Chardin's philosophy. On page 160 he states, "Now after a third of a century of service with the U.N. I can say unequivocally that much of what I have observed in the world bears out the all-encompassing, global, forward-looking philosophy of Teilhard de Chardin."[12] He claims that Teilhard viewed the U.N. as the institutional embodiment of his vision, and Muller himself believes that the human species is entering a new period of evolution, a period of planetary consciousness and global living, the birth of a collective brain.

Robert Muller, it is worth mentioning, has very close ties to Lucis Trust as well. (More on this later.) In his book he states,

> Was it not inevitable that the U.N. would sooner or later acquire a spiritual dimension . . . I have come to believe firmly today that our future peace, justice, fulfillment, happiness and harmony on this planet will not depend on world government but on divine or cosmic government, meaning that we must seek and apply the natural, evolutionary, divine, universal or cosmic laws which must rule our journey in the cosmos. Most of these laws can be found in the great religions and prophecies, and they are being rediscovered slowly but surely in the world organizations. Any Teilhardian will recognize in this the spiritual transcendence which he announced so emphatically as the next step in our evolution.[13]

In every chapter of *New Genesis*, Muller calls for a one world government and a one world religion as the only answer to mankind's problems. He completes his book with a prayer in which he tells humanity, "Be a cosmic, divine being, an integral, conscious part of the universe ... Be always open to the entire universe."[14] In his role as assistant secretary general, he was for many years in charge of the operations of thirty-two specialized agencies and world programs of the United Nations, including the Children's Fund (UNICEF), World Food Program, International Monetary Fund, International Labor Organization, and the U.N. Educational, Scientific and Cultural Organization (UNESCO). At this time, most of the funding for these various organizations comes from the United States (our tax dollars). Such is the influence of the disciples of Teilhard de Chardin.

Steeped in Pantheism

Carl Jung conceived his ideas of the collective unconscious or "race mind" by going within to the underground caverns of his own psyche. Chardin appears to do just the opposite. He looks at people, history and the world about him and discovers what he calls the "noosphere." This was his name for a vast global envelope of consciousness and shared thought surrounding the planet. In reality, both ideas are the same. In their view, we are not unique individuals, responsible for our own independent thoughts and choices, nor are we accountable to a personal God for those thoughts and choices. Rather, we are all part of a vast living organism (a global brain) that encompasses all of human-

ity and God as well. This is the essence of pantheistic religion.

Chardin sought to blend Christianity with
his ideas of the evolution of a "sacred earth" at
all costs, and Christian doctrine suffered greatly
in the process. The Apostle Paul certainly didn't
see Christ as an evolving entity, for he states in
Hebrew 13:8, "Jesus Christ the same yesterday,
and today, and for ever."

There are many beautiful passages in the
Bible which praise God for the wonders of His
creation and the beauty of the earth, but these
passages always direct our attention to God as
the source of creative power. Chardin's reverence, on the other hand, was always directed
toward the earth itself. He turned created matter into an idol and then worshipped that idol.
Romans 1:21-23 (NIV) reveals that man has fallen
for this delusion before:

> For although they knew God, they neither
> glorified him as God nor gave thanks to him,
> but their thinking became futile and their
> foolish hearts were darkened. Although they
> claimed to be wise, they became fools and
> exchanged the glory of the immortal God for
> images made to look like mortal man and
> birds and animals and reptiles.

Any study of witchcraft, whether one calls it
black or white witchcraft, will show the connection of these occult practices to the worship (or
invoking) of the "forces of nature." The modern
witchcraft movement is known as Wicca. These
people believe they derive their spiritual powers

from a mystical relationship with the earth. They live by the rhythms of the earth, moon and planets. The terms *Mother Earth* and *Mother Nature* are commonly used in modern day goddess-worship, which is so popular in current feminist, New Age circles.

Lucis Trust also promotes full moon meditations and helps people ·locate others in their area who are interested in such practices. And the National Organization of Women (NOW) has held conferences promoting these pagan/occultic concepts. For example, at their twentieth annual conference, held in Denver in June of 1986, one of their workshops was on Feminist Spirituality—The Goddess Returns.

These groups feel quite comfortable with many of the spiritual teachings of Teilhard de Chardin and Carl Jung. We know there are an abundance of institutions which are actively promoting these teachings of false hope. Like the Institute of Carl Jung in Switzerland, there is a foundation in Paris for the study of Chardin's works; the Teilhard Center for the Future of Man is located in London. There is also a Teilhard Foundation in Boulder, Colorado.

Evolving Toward Omega Point

Teilhard de Chardin saw every aspect of existence, from the earth itself to human beings, as moving in a purposeful forward, upward motion to his concept of the Omega Point. For him, Christogenesis, the movement by which the universe turns completely into Christ, is simply the last phase of evolution. He presented to the people of his day a religion which he still tried to call Christian. But the result was in every sense a vehicle for moving theologically into a new mindset which accepts a futuristic view of a supposed golden New Age to come. This age would, of course, be ushered in by man's own efforts.

Teilhard believed he was giving the world a better Christianity, which blended faith in God with faith in the world. He referred to this as the birth of a new faith. In an essay entitled, "The Stuff of the Universe," he makes this very clear.

> One could say that a hitherto unknown form of religion . . . is gradually germinating in the heart of modern man, in the furrow opened up by the idea of evolution . . . Far from feeling my faith perturbed by such a profound change, it is with hope overflowing that I welcome the rise of this new mystique and foresee its inevitable triumph.[15]

Like the other three people we have studied who have been used to lay the foundation for the New Age movement of today, Chardin seems to have been heavily influenced by the pantheistic concepts and beliefs of the East. While they spent time in India, he spent time first in Egypt, and then many years in China. He came to believe that we are all in the process of experiencing a spiritually upward evolution (as well as a physical evolution), and that at our Omega Point, we will also become a united humanity in this spiritual sense. Some New Agers refer to this final step of evolution as "taking a quantum leap." Chardin states,

> A tendency towards unification is everywhere manifest, and especially in the different branches of religion. We are looking for something that will draw us together, below or above the level of that which divides . . . Is our dilemma insoluble or (as we would rather believe) only a temporary one, destined to vanish like so many others when we have reached a higher level of spiritual evolution.[16]

The fact is, Christianity is completely unique and is the exact opposite of every manmade religion on earth. In every case, without exception, when an attempt is made to blend it with the religions of the world, it is Christianity that suffers and ceases to be what it is truly meant to be. Chardin never presents sin, redemption, Christ's shed blood or the nature of the Atonement in their proper perspective. Perhaps this failure to deal with the reality of sin and man's fallen nature is why his brand of spirituality is so appealing to the human potential advocates of today. Second Timothy 4:3-4 would confirm this:

> For the time will come when they will not endure sound doctrine; but after their own lusts shall they heap to themselves teachers, having itching ears; And they shall turn away their ears from the truth, and shall be turned unto fables.

The Apostle Paul's priorities were far different from Chardin's, for he tells the Corinthians,

> For I delivered unto you first of all that which
> I also received, how that Christ died for our
> sins according to the scriptures; And that he
> was buried, and that he rose again the third
> day according to the scriptures. (1 Cor. 15:3-4)

Pierre Teilhard de Chardin died on 10 April 1955, Easter Sunday, in New York City. After collapsing suddenly, he regained consciousness for a few moments. His last words were, "This time, I feel it's terrible."[17] A work entitled *My Litany* was found on his desk at the time of his death. The last lines of this litany indicate that Chardin stayed true to his beliefs to the end of his life: "Focus of ultimate and universal energy, centre of the cosmic sphere of cosmogenesis, Heart of Jesus, heart of evolution, unite me to yourself."[18]

If Chardin were alive today, I believe he would immediately be struck by two things. The first would be how incredibly popular his ideas have become. And the second is how wrong his predictions of our golden future were. Since his death in 1955, man has not been on an upward spiral, but just the opposite. Our globe is experiencing at this moment more wars, physical oppression, racial hatred, crime and terrorism than ever before in human history. The horrors of child pornography, drug abuse, abortion and the pandemic of AIDS hardly indicate an upward move of humanity.

The Bible tells us that man was originally created perfect and was placed in a perfect environment. His rebellion against a personal God has set him on a downward spiral ever since. And it is not an "evolving Christ" who can lift us out of this dilemma. Jesus, as we have already seen, compared the time prior to his return to the condition of mankind in the days of Noah, which was hardly an upward move toward omega either. God has given the world His solution for our predicament, but many (like Chardin), through pride and pseudo-intellectualism, reject it as being too naive.

God's solution is to forgive us of our sins and to grant us eternal life in heaven. However, we must first accept the fact that Jesus paid the penalty for our sins by dying on the cross in our place.

> God was in Christ, reconciling the world unto himself, not imputing their trespasses unto them . . . For he hath made him to be sin for us, who knew no sin; that we might be the righteousness of God in him. (2 Cor. 5:19, 21)

We will not reach the Omega Point in human history by all being absorbed into a universal Christ (a myth), but rather by kneeling in repentance at the feet of Him who said, "I am Alpha and Omega, the beginning and the end, the first and the last" (Rev. 22:13).

Chapter Three

◇

The Facade of Global Unity

Thus saith the Lord of hosts, Hearken not unto the words of the prophets that prophesy unto you: they make you vain: they speak a vision of their own heart, and not out of the mouth of the Lord.

—Jeremiah 23:16

These have one mind, and shall give their power and strength unto the beast.

—Revelation 17:13

During the 1980s, when I first considered writing on what was happening in the spiritual world of the New Age movement, I had no idea of the magnitude of what I was about to discover, especially concerning those developments designed to bring about a false sense of global peace and unity. The Bible says much about the power of unity, but it is a different kind of unity from that being advocated by today's globalists.

In Jesus' high priestly prayer in the seven-

99

teenth chapter of John, He prayed to the Father that His followers might "be one" and said that the result of this unity would be that the world would know the Father had sent Him to be its Savior. It doesn't take much discernment to see that the defeat of this type of true unity has been one of Satan's main objectives for the last two thousand years. Satan is not a creator; but he is the world's greatest counterfeiter. And, as we will see, he certainly has been hard at work in recent years through the efforts of many New Age leaders, to bring about some of the greatest human unity events in world history.

Satan tried to unify humanity once before on the plain of Shinar which is in modern day Iraq (Gen. 11:1-9) by erecting a great tower to the glory of man, apparently through his servant Nimrod. This ancient temple tower, or ziggurat, was not only intended to serve as a rallying point to unite all of humanity but is also believed to have been an occult worship site, probably the first of its kind. Then, as now, Satan works through human leaders who have rejected the true knowledge of God in favor of a religion that glorifies and deifies mankind.

Nimrod was the first man, at least of the post-Flood era, who desired to set himself up as a ruler over other people (Gen. 10:8-12). He founded the ancient centers of Babylon and Nineveh which any Bible student would equate with idol worship, promiscuous immorality and violence. While the memory of God's judgment via the Flood was still fresh in humanity's mind,

Nimrod became, as the ancient Septuagint translation of the Old Testament states, "a mighty hunter against the Lord."

> All tradition from the earliest times bears testimony to the apostasy of Nimrod and to his success in leading men away from the patriarchal faith and delivering their minds from that awe of God and fear of the judgment of heaven.[1]

The fallen nature of man seems more than willing to rally around anyone who can offer them a system of salvation and earthly utopia without a repentant heart and a reverence for a personal God to whom they are accountable.

John Randolph Price and World Healing Day

Unfortunately, this world still has its Nimrods. One of them is John Randolph Price, founder of the Quartus Foundation in Austin, Texas. In his book, *The Planetary Commission*, he lays out the blueprint for humanity to take its "quantum leap" into the golden New Age, where "mankind will return to Godkind." This is to be the Omega Point of human evolution. Instructed by his spirit guide, Asher, J.R. Price planned the greatest anti-God endeavor since the Tower of Babel. World Healing Day on 31 December 1986, was a massive worldwide event, deceptively portrayed as a coming together of humanity to usher in world peace.

By the time this book is in its final form, more than eight years will have come and gone since that event, but its effects have remained with us. For example, it helped inspire other human unity events, such as the Rio de Janeiro Earth Summit in 1992, and the Parliament of World Religions Conference in 1993; an example of just two events organized by some of the same people. By dissecting and analyzing the philosophy and theology behind World Healing Day we can gain much insight into the thinking of today's New Age spiritual leaders.

John Price began his quest on the metaphysical path in 1967 out of a sense of restlessness in life and a desire to discover something more. His quest led him deeply into New Age mysticism and he eventually became a featured speaker on the Unity Church and New Thought circuits.

In his 1981 book, *The Super Beings*, he states,

> It has been said that behind all fiction is a basis of fact. Does this mean that there is a grain of truth in the fictional Superman? What did the original creator of this comic strip and movie character have in mind when he first conceived the idea? Did he intuitively believe that man may someday evolve into a super-human creature with "out of this world" powers? If so, he was right.[2]

He goes on to say,

> Modern Science reports that the entire universe is made up of energy. The Illumined Ones tell us that this Energy is in reality the One Presence and Power of the universe—all Knowing, all-Loving, everywhere present, and

that this pure Mind Energy is individualized
in man, as man.[3]

Notice how quickly he moves from a fact of
science to a statement from the "Illumined
Ones." It is important to understand from this
point on, that the writings of John Price and the
plan for World Healing Day were "spiritually"
directed. The subtle and deceptive nature of
this worldwide event was truly diabolical when
we realize that it was sold to the public as a
great appeal for world peace, when in reality it
was designed to launch the eventual elimination
of everyone who doesn't buy into its occultic
plan.

Achieving Critical Mass

According to John Price, as informed by
Asher, 1987 was to be the year of critical mass
of negative thought patterns. Mind power is everything according to this theology. So we, as
collective humanity, have the negative power to
cause wars, famines, tornados and even violent
crime. When enough people think negative
"black thoughts" it affects the entire planet and
influences the actions of other people.

This is what is popularly known in New Age
circles as "the Hundredth Monkey" concept. According to this analogy, there were ninety-nine
monkeys on a certain tropical island. One day a
monkey learned to wash her sweet potato before eating it. Soon she taught another monkey
to do the same and eventually all ninety-nine
monkeys on this particular island were washing

their sweet potatoes. The monkeys had taken an evolutionary "quantum leap" into a higher state of consciousness, and now this new pattern had been established in the "race mind" of monkeys. Simultaneously on the next island, without any personal contact, the hundredth monkey began washing its sweet potato. Price says,

> Because we are all related and connected on the subjective level, every single impulse in consciousness is impressed and registered in the collective consciousness of mankind—the universal energy field referred to as the race mind.[4]

Does anyone begin to see Carl Jung's teachings in all of this?

Thus far in human history, according to this concept, the mass of dark energy in the race mind has been subcritical in that the chain reaction of negative consequences has not been self-sustaining. Positive light has been released in the past by the appearance of Spiritual Masters which penetrated the darkness. Jesus, by their estimation, was only one of these great masters.

John Price and his spirit guide Asher called for this worldwide, mass meditation, in order to reverse the polarity of the force field and achieve a critical mass of positive energy. He believed that if fifty million people would meditate simultaneously and release their energies into the earth's magnetic field, the entire vibration of the planet would begin to change. That is why this event was set up to take place at the same hour all over the world. A timetable given on page 155 of *The Planetary Commission* revealed that the event was coordinated according to noon, Greenwich time. If you live in Moscow you would have meditated at 3 P.M.; Tokyo, 9 P.M.; Honolulu, 2 A.M.; Denver, 5 A.M.; and so on throughout the world.

They were also hoping for five hundred million people to give their mental consent for the healing of the planet through this process. This should "not only maintain the negative energy mass in a sub-critical state, but will also begin to break up the severe intensity of the 'dark pockets,' thus preparing the collective consciousness for the massive penetration of Light on the final day of 1986." Price believed that if this endeavor was successful, "this world can be transformed into a heaven right now."[5] If all of this sounds more like a wild science fiction movie than an actual event designed to change the world, let me reiterate that these people are deadly serious.

Planning for the Event

Not surprisingly, massive plans were made to insure the success of World Healing Day. The Quartus Foundation put out monthly updates on their activities in major cities across the United States and throughout the world. John Price stated,

> Millions more must be reached and influenced. Journalists must write about the Commission for the mass media. Those in broadcasting and film production must spread the

word. Every counselor, seminar leader, healer,
minister, practitioner, author, publisher, edu-
cator, teacher, and writer must speak and write
of the Commission. Every spiritual group must
rise above competitive attitudes and join together in a spirit of cooperation for world
healing . . . No conflict of philosophies should
keep us from supporting one another in this
endeavor.[6]

It seems obvious that any Bible-believing
Christian would have faced a most serious conflict of interest if asked to participate in the
events of World Healing Day, as the motives
and theology of the organizers ran diametrically
opposed to the teachings of the Bible. If there
is any remaining question about that, let me
quote from a book review given by Price in one
of his publications.

It should be pretty obvious that there is no
outer god who is about to yell, 'Whoa boys,
you've gone far enough; I'm coming down to
earth to take over and establish peace among
men and nations!' The God who is to save
mankind, if it is to be saved, is the divine
potential within humanity itself, the celestial
spark within each individual . . . There isn't
much doubt any longer that this Universe is
designed as a dwelling place for a race of
gods.[7]

According to the reports put out by the
Quartus Foundation, the Houston Astrodome
was used for this event. Other major centers
which were rented included McNichols Arena
in Denver (John Denver performing), Omni

Coliseum in Atlanta, the Metrodome in Minneapolis, the San Diego Stadium, and the University of New Mexico Sports Arena in Albuquerque. A New Ager in Kansas City stated their plans,

> We want to bring forth the creativity of Kansas City through music, visual arts, dance and drama with everything keyed off Teilhard de Chardin's line—"The future of the world is in our hands."[8]

In Alaska, one woman contacted several hundred churches by phone, stressing that World Healing Day crosses all religious and political lines so that everyone could participate. The Methodist Peace With Justice Task Force got the word out to all their Methodist churches in Alaska. One Lutheran minister carried the idea back to her seminary in the fall of 1986. The president of Alaska Pacific University made the information available to the students there.

The August 1986 report from Quartus claimed that eighteen African nations would be participating and that the entire population of Sri Lanka, fifteen million people, would be involved. A New Age couple in Israel organized an outreach group with the objective of uniting the entire state of Israel. New Age Communications Network of Australia stated that they were producing a fifty-minute television special called "Stop the Clock," which was to be tailored to support and help achieve the "critical mass of positive energy." And of course the New Age Light Center of Findhorn, Scotland, drew international attention to the commission through its publication "One Earth."

The Results

It appears that World Healing Day was somewhat more successful in other countries than it was in the United States. That may be due to the fact that a number of Christian ministries informed the public of the occultic nature of the event, revealed in some of the publicity materials that also emphasized peace and unity. Although the numbers may not have been as great as hoped for in some places, the media certainly did their part to promote the event. The *Seattle News Times* reported, "7000 Meditate On Peace In Seattle Kingdome"; *Peoria Journal Star*, "Peorians Light City in Instant of Cooperation Peace Vigil"; *Los Angeles Times*, "Hands Joined In Prayer All Around The Globe."[9] The January 1987 update from the Quartus Foundation claimed that twenty-three hundred people in Santa Cruz participated in a five hour program and twenty-five hundred in Kansas City heard Robert Muller reflect on the power of World Healing Day.

The foundation also reported that a total of seventy-seven countries and 524 organizations participated in this event. Plans were already underway for a "Second Annual Global Mind Link." John Price stated, "See you on December 31, 1987, noon Greenwich time—and on and on until everyone on Earth joins in and the last one comes into the Light."[10]

It is important to remember that all times and events are in God's hands and that these plans will only proceed until God intervenes. He stopped the Tower of Babel before it was completed by scattering the people and confusing their language. Psalm 2:1-4 says,

> Why do the heathen rage, and the people imagine a vain thing? The kings of the earth set themselves, and the rulers take counsel together, against the Lord, and against his anointed, saying, Let us break their bands asunder, and cast away their cords from us. He that sitteth in the heavens shall laugh: the Lord shall have them in derision.

Man always appears to seek a human or occult-based answer to his problem—anything but God's solution, or so it seems. In 1 Samuel, chapter 8, the people called to God to give them an earthly king so that they could be like the other nations around them. God said, "they have rejected me that I should not reign over them" (1 Sam. 8:7). Saul, the first king of Israel, instead of seeking God's counsel, became involved in the occult when he sought out the witch of Endor. The results were not very pleasant, and he soon lost his life.

A particular passage of Scripture puzzled me until a few years ago. One Thessalonians 5:3 states, "For when they shall say, Peace and safety; then sudden destruction cometh upon them, as travail upon a woman with child; and they shall not escape." I could never understand why destruction would come upon people who were saying peace and safety. But on 31 December 1986, and several times since, millions of people tried to manipulate world events through magic vibrations, summoning and empowering demonic spirits via occult meditation instead of interceding to the Prince of Peace through prayer. The prophet Jeremiah said, "For they have healed the hurt of the daughter of my people slightly, saying, Peace, peace; when there is no peace" (Jer. 8:11).

On page 157 of *The Planetary Commission*, John Price gave the World Healing Meditation which he hoped everyone would use during this transforming planetary hour. I share just a part of it here.

> Now is the time of the new beginning. I am a co-creator with God, and it is a new Heaven that comes as the Good Will of God is expressed on Earth through me . . . I begin with me. I am a living Soul and the Spirit of God dwells in me, as me. I and the Father are one, and all that the Father has is mine. In truth, I am the Christ of God . . . There is total Oneness, and in this Oneness we speak the Word. Let the sense of separation be dissolved. Let mankind be returned to Godkind.

In the past, we have had various cult leaders claiming to be "the Christ" or the new messiah, and some of them have gained large followings. Now we have witnessed millions of people at the same moment saying, "In truth, I am the Christ of God." Jesus warned in Luke 21:8, "Take heed that ye be not deceived: for many shall come in my name, saying, I am Christ; and the time draweth near: go ye not therefore after them." I can only add my "amen" to that.

Pressing toward Their Goal

In the previous chapter, I stated that the foundation stones for today's move toward a one world religion were carefully being laid during the last century. It would seem that John Price and I are in agreement about this timetable. On page one of *The Super Beings* he states,

> The revolution has begun. It started more than one hundred years ago, but now the pace is quickening. Throughout the world, men and women are joining in the uprising and are coming forward to be counted as part of a new race that will someday rule the universe.[11]

That rule which Price is speaking of will not be by a new race of super beings, but by a power-hungry elite who are integrating their ideas into our culture in subtle but powerful ways. "We Are the World" is not just a song but a theology. Human unity events are now the popular trend. We have had U.S.A. for Africa, Live Aid, Farm Aid, the Goodwill Games sponsored by Ted Turner, the First Earth Run and Hands Across America, to name just a few. These events have not just been humanitarian relief efforts, but incredible consciousness-raising gatherings to promote the idea of this planet as one living organism, an interdependent "spaceship earth."

Live Aid alone was allegedly seen by 1.5 billion people in 160 countries. That is one in every three people in the world. These events have shown how easy it is to draw massive numbers of people into such promotions. Organizers from the Planetary Commission had every reason to believe that World Healing Day would be the biggest in this series of events.

Big name entertainers had been brought in to draw large crowds for these events. Some of them were practicing New Agers. Willie Nelson, for example, was the featured performer on 4 July 1986, at Farm Aid at the Houston Astrodome. In a newspaper called *New Age Activist*, he talked about his strong belief in reincarnation.[12]

Harry Belafonte was the musician responsible for organizing the "We Are the World" concert and album which purportedly was designed to alleviate world hunger. However, in a later interview in *Billboard Magazine*, Belafonte pointed out that it really was just another part of the campaign to overthrow the present nation-state system and set up a U.N.-run world government.[13]

Broadcaster Ted Turner, at a New Age conference, stated that America must elect a New Age president if it wants to survive through the year 2000. He revealed that he has come to the conclusion that we (America) are the greatest problem in the world.[14] It seems that his "good will" does not extend to his own country, where the free enterprise system has enabled him to become a multimillionaire with his own T.V. stations reaching millions of American homes.

Billions to Be "Cleansed"

John Price claims that we have entered the New Age, but we now have the responsibility to create the civilization to go with it. This Aquarian Age will open its arms of welcome to all who embrace its new theology. However, those who take Jesus at His Word when He said, "I am the way, the truth, and the life: no man cometh unto the Father, but by me" (John 14:6) will need to experience a "cleansing" because of their self-centered, separatist ideas. The New Age idea of being selfish or self-centered is to believe that each person is an individual, who began their existence in time at the moment of conception, and to believe that they are a creature separate from their all-powerful creator. To be separatist is to refuse to believe that all the world's religions are so similar that there is no problem in fusing them into one harmonious whole.

The familiar spirit guide, Asher, explains this cleansing action in some detail to John Price on pages 18-19 of *Practical Spirituality*. John states he hopes that the building process of the Planetary Commission will be done in peace and harmony, and that the activities will result in a dramatic change for the good of all mankind. Asher seems to see things a bit differently. He states,

> This fusing of energies, which will reach a peak on December 31, 1986, will remove the threat of global war but will not eliminate all local hostilities. It will also cause dramatic advances in scientific discoveries, revamp the

concept of established 'religion and church,'
and serve as a ring of protection for more
than three billion people . . . Nature will soon
enter her cleansing cycle. Those who reject
the earth's changes with an attitude of 'it can't
happen here' will experience the greatest
emotion of fear and panic, followed by rage
and violent action. These individuals with their
lower vibratory rates, will be removed during
the next two decades.

Price then states, "I know that one of the
most serious problems we have today is over-
population, but wiping more than 2 billion
people off the face of the earth is a little drastic,
don't you think?" Asher replies, "Who are we to
say that these people did not volunteer to be a
part of the destruction and regeneration—for
the purpose of soul growth?"[15]

It appears that John Price has accepted
Asher's plans for planet earth. In a later report
from the Quartus Foundation, he discussed the
results of the massive world meditation:

Through the efforts of millions of men and
women with purity of motive and a consciousness reaching for Christhood, the world of
illusion will separate into islands of Light and
Darkness. Those attracted to the Light will
gather as one . . . and they shall be taken into
the Light and they will become the Light.
And the light shall spread to the island of
darkness and it will cease to exist.[16]

Reading this material is like reading *Screwtape
Letters* by C. S. Lewis. Everything is backwards
and reversed. The prophet Isaiah warned:

Woe unto them that call evil good, and good evil; that put darkness for light, and light for darkness; that put bitter for sweet, and sweet for bitter! . . . so their root shall be as rottenness, and their blossom shall go up as dust: because they have cast away the law of the Lord of hosts . . . (Isa. 5:20, 24)

So far in this chapter we have looked at how one man and his demon spirit guide influenced World Healing Day. An event of this magnitude, however, must have had the cooperation of a whole network of people. Let's turn our attention now to another individual who put much time and energy into making this event a success.

Barbara Marx Hubbard

Barbara Marx Hubbard is a pleasant-looking, gray-haired grandmother with an infectious smile, and an enthusiasm for her work in solving the world's problems that could put many Christians to shame. She is, however, also blinded by the great deceiver of the minds of men and nations (Rev. 20:2, 3) and is unfortunately leading thousands of other people with her along the path of darkness.

Her list of credentials and her scope of influence reads like a *Who's Who In America*. Barbara is the daughter of the late toy manufacturer Louis Marx. She graduated from Bryn Mawr College, cum laude in political science, and in 1970, co-founded the Committee for the Future with John Whiteside. She is on the board of directors of the World Future Society, which sponsored the conference Worldview 84. (A forum composed of the top world government advocates, which served as a platform for the World Constitution and Parliament Association.)

Hubbard is also a former member of the Presidential Committee on National Curriculum, and she was a Democratic party nominee for the vice-presidency of the United States in 1984. (This was the same convention that Gov. Mario Cuomo addressed.) She is the founder of the New World Center in Washington, D.C., and has been an advisor to such organizations as the Federal Energy Administration, the House of Representatives and the Senate. She produces a radio program called "New News from the Peace Room" which is an "international radio outreach for 'IT'—the whole field of people who contain within them the planetary DNA—the next step in evolution."[17] She resides in Gainesville, Florida, where she has been working with Hazel Henderson, the global environmentalist/economist.

A Major Organizer

Through her initiative, the Human Unity Conference established a subgroup of forty people who made contact with the heads of all religious groups in the world to encourage support of World Healing Day. Barbara spread the word in her workshops, lectures and international travels. In the spring of 1986, she made a trip to the Soviet Union with eighty other

American "citizen diplomats" to engage in dialogue with their counterparts on the theme "In Search of a Positive Future." While there, she discovered that Joseph Goldin, a Moscow writer who supposedly had never heard of the Planetary Commission, was working on an event for New Year's Eve 1986 which was almost identical to John Price's World Healing Day.

Joseph Goldin says,

> Who would write a script for a global New Year's Party involving two billion people participants? After the success of the global Live Aid Concert on 13 July 1985, which brought together a phenomenal worldwide audience to match the importance of the event, a global New Year's Party with a focal point in Moscow is not so wild a dream. Still, how does one go about writing a script for such a mega-vision? People on different continents will be thrilled by experiencing a sense of distant proximity and might gladly go along with lighting candles. As a result, two billion people across the globe will see one another via space bridges.[18]

Needless to say, Barbara and Joseph began working together.

Goldin received help for international communication from Yevgeny Velikhou, vice-president of the Soviet Academy of Sciences. Velikhou was involved with Mikhail Gorbachev's drive to widen the use of computers in the USSR. The U.S. Department of Commerce had reportedly already given the go-ahead for computer links to Goldin's U.S. contacts. Ted Turner and a

"Moscow faith healer" had talked on the system. It appears that Joseph Goldin targeted the 31 December Peace Event as a major focus for his electronic exchanges. Arrangements were also worked out with MTV (Music Television) to set up a seven continent global television link-up, similar to the one set up for Live Aid.

Reinterpreting the Bible

Barbara Marx Hubbard referred to 31 December 1986, as a "Planetary Pentecost" where participants would have the powers of Christ to heal, resurrect the dead and even transform their physical bodies as Christ transformed His, at that instant or in the twinkling of an eye. She teaches that we are all brain cells of the global brain. By holding, connecting and sharing it (the global brain), we will unlock the key to the planetary shift in consciousness, or take the "quantum leap" in spiritual evolution, toward reaching our own godhood.

Her explanation of what happened on the day of Pentecost in the Upper Room to the 120 followers of Jesus is most interesting.

> I believe a magnetic field of consciousness was created which activated the dormant powers, which exist in each of us. They became fearless and were transfigured by resonance, unconditional love, which provided a field in which to experience Spirit collectively. A Planetary Pentecost would be a mass transfiguration and empowerment of millions at once . . . a "second coming" through lifting our own consciousness to Christ-centered consciousness.[19]

This concept certainly dovetails perfectly with John Price's occultic explanation of the Second Coming of Christ (which is, in reality, his explanation of the emergence of the anti-Christ world system). He describes the return of Christ as a new energy field which will seed human consciousness, causing it to become the Christ individualized. Who will experience this kind of a second coming? Mrs. Hubbard tells us that we cannot reach the "Tree of Life," the Tree of Immortality in a state of self-centered consciousness, laboring under the illusion that we are separate. The power we are inheriting is too great for a self-centered species.

Barbara has written her own interpretation of the book of Revelation called *Manual for Co-Creators of the Quantum Leap*. In her book, *The Evolutionary Journey*, she gives us some background information which led to the writing of this material. She tells us, "All my life I have been a seeker for meaning. Born of a Jewish agnostic, affluent background in 1929, I received no spiritual training." Her "seeking" led her down many paths until she read *The Phenomenon of Man* by Teilhard de Chardin. She claims,

> It was an epiphany for me. There is a continuing, evolving pattern in the process of nature that leads to greater whole systems, higher consciousness and freedom . . . and it's going on NOW. Its unfinished. The world is evolving, not just the individual. Not only do I have unused growth potential . . . so does the world . . . so does our species . . . and so does the universe! Something new is coming.

The magnetic attraction was right. I could
trust my intuition.[20]

After this she sought out people throughout
the world who were working on aspects of our
next step forward and who felt the attraction
that Teilhard describes.

The problem at this point, from Barbara's
perspective, was that humanity was still self-centered, suffering from the illusion of separation
from God. Remember, that according to New
Age theology, to be self-centered and separatist
is to believe that you are a sinful creature in
need of the grace of a personal God . . . which,
in reality, describes a God-centered, not a self-
centered, life. New Agers turn everything upside down; it is they who are self-centered by
seeking their own personal empowerment and
liberation from a personal God, rather than
seeking to serve and love Him who is the Author and Creator of all things (and who knows
what is best for us).

Hearing from the Other Side

In a state of frustration, Hubbard rented a
house in Santa Barbara in January of 1980 to
write a book on the evolutionary perspective.
Near a monastery, she claimed to hear the voice
of Jesus telling her, "My resurrection was a sig-
nal for all of yours." At this point, Barbara Marx
Hubbard was about to make the mistake of her
life. Nearly two thousand years ago the Apostle
Paul warned about listening to this voice.

> I am amazed that you are so quickly deserting Him who called you by the grace of Christ for a different gospel.... But even though we, or an angel from heaven should preach to you a gospel contrary to that which we have preached to you, let him be accursed.... And no wonder, for even Satan disguises himself as an angel of light. (Gal. 1:6, 8; 2 Cor. 11:14, NAS)

The following is a sample of what this "angel of light" has revealed through a willing human channel:

> The communion ceremony is to become the union ceremony ... As each person has a higher, wiser self, so does the species-as-a-whole.... Be members of a more mature species. You HAVE THE POWERS OF A NATURAL CHRIST. This is what I came to Earth to reveal ... Yours are the powers. Yours the glory. You—all of you who are desirous and ready—are the way. Be a beacon of light unto yourselves. This tiny band, this brave congregation of souls attracted to the future of the world are my avant-garde, my new order of the future. They are self-selected souls who have come to earth to carry the miracle of the resurrection into action as the transformation of Homo sapiens to Homo universalist.[21]

Barbara shares with the reader some of her reactions and thoughts as these revelations were given to her.

> The floodgates of my mind had opened. It was as if an unseen hand was activating the memory bank of my brain. I organized noth-

ing. I "thought" of nothing. I simply recorded
the stream of ideas . . . Sometimes a voice that
called itself "Jesus" interpreted authoritative-
ly. . . . In other passages it seemed as though
the voices were those of our elder brothers
and sisters who have gone before and already
know the way. I feel that "I"—my normal waking, conscious personality, who has been a
seeker—virtually co-created the text with a hierarchy of other, higher selves . . . Other sec-
tions seemed to come from a collective species consciousness.[22]

Destruction of the Old Order

Mrs. Hubbard sees the New Testament as a
book of instructions for the final countdown to
birth, the selection of the God-centered from
the self-centered. She claims that the Book of
Revelation is a last statement from God to earth-
bound, self-centered humanity, revealing details
of the tribulation to come and a glimpse of the
New Jerusalem which we are to build.

These various "voices" stand ready to give
the world their interpretation of the sixth chapter of Revelation; and we are to believe that the
chosen vessel for this revelation is a woman with
practically no previous biblical knowledge, no
background in Hebrew or Greek or any other
biblical scholarship. Her only claim is that up
until now, she has been confused and seeking
for answers. What follows sounds very much
like a conversation between Woodworm and
Uncle Screwtape, the fictitious demon characters of C. S. Lewis.

Of Revelation 6:4 they say,

> Humanity will not be able to make the transition from Earth-only to universal life until the chaff has been separated from the wheat. The great reaper must reap before we can take the quantum leap to the next phase of evolution. No worldly peace can prevail until the self-centered members of the planetary body either change or die. That is the choice. The red horse is the destruction during the birth process of those who refuse to be born into God-centered, universal life . . . This act is as horrible as killing a cancer cell. It must be done for the sake of the future of the whole. So be it: be prepared for the selection process which is now beginning. The second seal revealed a red horse ridden by one with the power to take peace from the Earth. It stands for the necessity of the selection process which shall rip apart the old order and destroy those who choose to remain self-centered remnants of the past.[23]

Barbara Hubbard would have done well to read the first chapter of Revelation, where the Apostle John tells us that Jesus is the Ruler of the kings of the earth and the One who releases us from our sins by His blood (Rev. 1:5). Instead, she continues to listen to the voices that tell a different story. Let's take a look at what these voices have to say about those who are fulfilling Jesus' command to take the gospel into all the world. "The modern moralists who preach the irremediable degradation of human beings as sinners are assassinating the witnesses to hope . . . But even now my legions are growing."

She goes on to mock and counter true Christians, saying,

> Evangelists are proclaiming that the kingdom of God is at hand. They are urging repentance and acceptance of Jesus as your personal savior. . . . It is your work to envision the New Jerusalem as a society of full humanity wherein each person is a natural Christ. Dearly beloveds, you are my New Order for the future.[24]

Of the New Jerusalem, my Bible tells me something very different. "And the city had no need of the sun, neither of the moon, to shine in it: for the glory of God did lighten it, and the Lamb is the light thereof" (Rev. 21:23). This same Lamb is the One who is in full control of all the events of the sixth chapter of Revelation. He is the One who breaks the seals in verses 1, 3, 5, 7, 9 and 12. He also later breaks the seventh seal in Revelation 8:1. Who is this Lamb? John the Baptist identifies Him for us, "The next day John seeth Jesus coming unto him, and saith, 'Behold the Lamb of God, which taketh away the sins of the world' " (John 1:29).

Mrs. Hubbard's demon voices continue their reverse scenario of the tribulation.

> We, the elders, have been patiently waiting until the very last moment before the quantum transformation, to take action to cut out this corrupted and corrupting element in the body of humanity. It is like watching a cancer grow; something must be done before the whole body is destroyed . . . the self-centered members must be destroyed. There is no al-

ternative. Only the God-centered can evolve.
Fortunately you, dearly beloveds, are not responsible for this act. We are. We are in
charge of God's selection process for planet
Earth. He selects, we destroy. We are the rid-
ers of the pale horse, Death. We will use whatever means we must to make this act of destruction as quick and painless as possible to
the one-half of the world who are capable of
evolving . . . Now everything is global and connected. Each person is about to inherit the
power of destruction and co-creation. The
inner voice, the higher self, each person's own
connection to God—independent of priest,
text, church or mentor—must be heard
directly . . . Those of you who know what is
happening—the one-fourth who are now listening to the higher self—are to be guides for
the rest who will be panicked and confused.[25]

Notice that "the elders" want to make this
destruction painless, not for those who are being destroyed, but for those who will have to
witness the destruction, the so-called God-centered co-creators. This material goes on for
pages, but I think this has shown a clear picture
of the mindset of Mrs. Hubbard and the voices
that guide her.

It is clear to anyone who has studied the
writings of Pierre Teilhard de Chardin that
Barbara Marx Hubbard is one of his disciples.
Talk of quantum transformation, spiritual evolution, and everything being globally connected
puts her right into the heart of this theology.

There is a strong warning at the end of the
Book of Revelation that Barbara would have

done well to read before she began this odyssey into distortion. Revelation 21:5 says, "And he that sat upon the throne said, Behold, I make all things new. And he said unto me, Write: for these words are true and faithful." Barbara states, "Here is what I recorded in response to this verse. And he who sat upon the throne said to me, 'Behold I am writing anew, through scribes on earth who are willing to listen to me.' "[26]

One thing we can know about our all-powerful, all-knowing God is that He does not contradict Himself. Here is what He said two thousand years ago and it still applies.

> For I testify unto every man that heareth the words of the prophecy of this book, If any man shall add unto these things, God shall add unto him the plagues that are written in this book: And if any man shall take away from the words of the book of this prophecy, God shall take away his part out of the book of life, and out of the holy city, and from the things, which are written in this book. (Rev. 22:18-19)

Other "Peace" Events of the Eighties

It seems that 1986 was the year of megapeace events. World Healing Day on 31 December 1986 was not a single event, but rather a climax to a series of events, designed to shift our consciousness into viewing the world as one harmonious whole. Another of these events was called the Million Minutes of Peace. I first learned about this endeavor through a mailing which I received from Lucis Trust, the organization which supports and promotes the works of Alice Bailey.

Million Minutes of Peace

Million Minutes of Peace puts out a monthly newsletter called "Minute By Minute." In the first issue of their newsletter they stated, "What started out as a project for the United Nations International Year of Peace in Australia has mushroomed into a global initiative with over 40 countries taking part." They also have a publication called "Your Thoughts Count" which explains that their aim is to collect pledges, not of money, but of thoughts of peace. This "Million Minutes" ran from 16 September to 16 October 1986.

The promoters stated that people were prepared to commit themselves to link with others in thought, regardless of belief, tradition or political differences. On page two of their first issue, they talked about the "hundredth monkey" concept and went on to say,

> There are two prerequisites: First, pure thought must be sustained over a relatively long period. Second, a critical number of people must think thoughts of peace in order for the thought pattern to become common awareness.

The appeal was launched in the foyer of the United Nations and the U.N. chapel was open from noon to five o'clock for people to donate their minutes of peace.

The list of groups and individuals, which either endorsed this event or actively worked for its success, included Lucis Trust, Eileen Caddy (co-founder of Findhorn), His Holiness the Dalai Lama, Institute of Noetic Sciences (Willis Harman), Friends of the Earth, Planetary Citizens, Brahma Kumanis World Spiritual Organization, author Sydney Sheldon, Rt. Hon. Bishop Desmond Tutu, author/lecturer Marilyn Ferguson, Sen. Edward Kennedy, the president of the World Council of Churches, the Church of Religious Science, Unity-in-Diversity Council, and the Human Unity Institute, to name just a few.

> The Appeal climaxed at a Peace Concert that was held at St. John the Divine Cathedral in Manhattan. An estimated ten thousand people watched as the final count of the minutes donated worldwide was presented to Dr. James O.C. Jonah, assistant Secretary General of the United Nations. A candle lighting ceremony symbolized the minds' pledges of peaceful thought.[27]

This is the same cathedral that displays a female Christ on the cross, complete with shapely hips and full breasts. The Very Reverend James Parks Morton, dean of the Cathedral stated that the response to the crucifix was very positive. One wonders how far blasphemy can go. "Her prophets are light and treacherous persons: her priests have polluted the sanctuary, they have done violence to the law" (Zeph. 3:4).

Peace the 21st

In another mailing from Lucis Trust I learned about "Peace the 21st." This outreach is being organized on the twenty-first day of the months that represent the change of seasons: March, June, September and December. An Indiana member of the "Love of Peace Alliance" stated that since the goal is to transform the planet, it makes sense to meet on the days when the earth undergoes natural changes. They believe that the collective thought of the human race might be the most powerful force in the world. Guided meditations are a part of their meetings. Over one hundred peace poles have been erected around the country as well, to cause people to think and meditate on peace. "May Peace Prevail On Earth" is written in four different languages on these poles.

A toll-free number was given for those who wanted more information about Peace the 21st. When a friend called the number listed, the operator who answered was taking pledges for Hands Across America. It appeared that these two groups were working together. The U.S.A. for Africa Foundation was the sponsor of Hands Across America and We Are The World. Hands Across America united approximately six million people allegedly to solve one of the world's greatest problems of hunger.

It is not my intention to undermine efforts to alleviate the suffering of the hungry or those in dire poverty. I am aware of many organizations, particularly Christian ones, who have been at the forefront of helping those in need, and have supported some of them. My concern, however, is with the motivation behind these massive unity events, which seem to be designed to subtly lead us into a one-world political, economic and religious system.

The First Earth Run

In 1986, we also experienced the First Earth Run. The purpose of the First Earth Run was supposedly to unite people all around the world in igniting a global sense of hope for the future. A contribution of five hundred dollars entitled one to carry the torch for a kilometer along the planned around-the-world path. UNICEF was the beneficiary of any excess proceeds from the project. The torch left the U.N. on 16 September (the launch date for Million Minutes of Peace) and was passed to thousands of runners before returning. The torch was to return to the United Nations on New Year's Eve, but because of financial difficulties, it was returned somewhat sooner. This demonstrated that most of the world's people had not yet "caught the vision."

The Harmonic Convergence

On 16-22 August 1987 the World Congress on Illumination held a meeting of twenty-five hundred "light workers" in Honolulu, Hawaii, in conjunction with the Harmonic Convergence celebrations held globally on 16 August. Patricia Diane Cota-Robles, president of the New Age

Study of Humanity's Purpose stated in her 4 March 1987 newsletter,

> There are many indications from ancient calendars and present day inner guidance that August 17, 1987 is a day of utmost significance. We have been guided from within to organize a global activity at that time that will serve as a vehicle through which Light Workers from all over the world can come together to meet each other and form a unified cup. This activity will be held with the force-field of Peace and Harmony that pulsates at Diamond Head in Hawaii.[28]

An afternoon workshop at this conference was entitled "Workshop and Guided Visualization to Energize our Unified Chalice of Service." One cannot help but be reminded of God's description of the false religion of the last days. Revelation 17:4 states: "And the woman was arrayed in purple and scarlet colour, and decked with gold and precious stones and pearls, having a golden cup in her hand full of abominations and filthiness of her fornication."

An organization in Boulder, Colorado, known as Harmonic Convergence had this to say about the August event.

> Harmonic Convergence is a conscious bonding of people to support an evolutionary shift from separation to unity and from fear to love. At the core, 144,000 people will gather at sunrise on August 16 at sacred sites around the globe. They will join at these Earth 'acupuncture points' to create a resonating link between Universal Energies and the Earth.[29]

Here we see a blending of New Age ideas—of an evolutionary shift in consciousness—with Oriental beliefs in the earth's energy, as expressed in acupuncture, and with plain old-fashioned witchcraft. Their desire to "express unity with all life" (which includes animals) and their emphasis on sites of pagan worship around the world make this obvious.

The people who organized this event are familiar with the Book of Revelation, but have distorted its meaning and are trying to bring about its fulfillment to conform with their own theology. The choosing of 144,000 people (Rev. 7:4) and the reference to a "unified cup" (Rev. 17:4) leave little doubt of their intent.

Globalism in Government

Since the late 1980s, this barrage of human unity events has only accelerated, crossing over into the political realm where New Age ideas have become fashionable among some of our top leaders. We are seeing today a strong blending of spiritual and political ideas in Washington. Our last two presidents have advocated world unity through an empowered United Nations, while knowingly, or unknowingly, using occult phrases such as "New World Order" and "a thousand points of light"—concepts promoted by Lucis Trust and the secret societies.

George Bush, a former director of the Council on Foreign Relations and member of the Trilateral Commission, became the first U.S. president to openly endorse the principles of the New World Order. By the time he left office, he had significantly enhanced the role of the United Nations in world affairs. This began with the Persian Gulf War and ended with Bush giving U.N. troops access to many U.S. military bases. Along the way, he launched the push to ratify NAFTA (the North American Free Trade Agreement). This regional economic trading block is intended to eventually become a political union, similar to the European union. North America is destined to become one of ten regions under the new world government, based on the Club of Rome's model (see p. 42, *En Route to Global Occupation*). The American people voted President Bush out of office, I believe, largely because of his preoccupation with foreign affairs and building the New World Order, which came at the expense of our national sovereignty and important domestic concerns.

However, to the surprise of many Americans, we got more of the same with Bill Clinton, except in a larger dose. President Clinton, like Bush, has been a member of the influential, pro-U.N., Council on Foreign Relations and Trilateral Commission. Since his term in office he has promoted gay rights, socialized medicine, an unconstitutional crime bill, and the ratification of all types of U.N. treaties, the latest of which is GATT (General Agreement on Tariffs and Trade); which establishes the new World Trade Organization (WTO), a huge international bureaucracy, to regulate the flow of trade.

The global organizations being created to oversee the implementation of NAFTA and GATT, not only diminish our national sovereignty while increasing the influence of the U.N., but will ultimately necessitate a world tax. These new agencies of the emerging world government have to be funded somehow. It seems that no price is too great if it helps bring about the illusion of progress toward "world peace and unity." In the meantime, the United States is approaching bankruptcy from its burgeoning federal debt. The ratification of GATT will only add to our deficit problem as it will eliminate billions of dollars of import tariffs each year.

While Bill Clinton has been busy promoting the New World Order, Vice-President Al Gore has entrenched himself in the global environmental movement, defending the rights of the spotted owl at the expense of thousands of jobs in the lumber industry. In the meantime millions of babies continue to be aborted, but the so-called rights of women to extinguish human life are upheld. It is fair to say that the laws now governing our land, in many cases, value animal life more than human life. It is not difficult for a New Ager, such as Al Gore, to embrace such values; since pantheists believe that on Mother Earth all life is one, and is part of the god force.

According to this belief system, humans are no more important than plants or animals. Al Gore's pantheistic views, although disguised under a thin veneer of Christian terminology, were reflected in his book, *Earth in the Balance*.

Gore's views were also evident in his strong support of the U.N. Summit on Population and Development in Cairo, which defended abortion in the name of population control.

The American people once again reflected their dismay with our leaders at the polls in 1994. Fed up with talk of world government, an empowered U.N., and the continued overseas involvement of our troops under U.N. command, most Americans I have spoken with want our national sovereignty defended and our freedoms restored. They want less government and would like the erosion of our domestic strength halted. It appears as if many people are finally waking up!

I can only hope that the latest elections will lead to the kinds of changes this nation desperately needs . . . a move away from world government, a reduction in spending, lower taxes, and the restoration of some of our personal freedoms which have been eroded during the last few years. A number of the newly elected Congressmen truly appear to be conservative in their views and will seek to uphold the Constitution while, hopefully, providing some much needed moral leadership. However, their efforts may soon be frustrated as they discover that some of the key bottleneck positions in Congress are still held by politicians with a pro-U.N., globalist view.

God's Unity

We know that God desires there to be love and unity among Christian believers. Earlier we mentioned Jesus' prayer for unity of spirit among His followers, demonstrating this fact. However, God's idea of unity is drastically different from the type of unity being pursued by the New Age of today. His Holy Spirit is moving across the face of the earth to bring about not a structural unity under a world government but a spiritual unity among all those who truly love and seek to obey Jesus Christ.

God's unity is not one that is organized or orchestrated but rather is something that results naturally among those who unselfishly love and seek the truth. The Bride of Christ, unfortunately a minority in this world, is being prepared for the great Marriage Supper of the Lamb, spoken of in Revelation 19:7-8. Jesus is coming back for a bride, not divided, but one united and having no spot, wrinkle or blemish; one that is holy and blameless (Eph. 5:27). She will have a heart devoted to her Bridegroom, Jesus Christ, not to her "holy Christ self."

Chapter Four

◆

Deceptions of a Post-Christian Era

If the foundations be destroyed, what can the righteous do?

—Psalm 11:3

The New Age movement seems to have much in common with termites. Termites work quietly and unseen, eating away at the foundation of structures. By the time the damage is noticed, it may be so extensive that major repairs or even drastic rebuilding measures are needed for the original structure to be saved.

Some groups are presently at the point of examining the building and are discovering that some damage has been done. The extent of that damage might shock and surprise most Christians.

Europe was once the scene of spiritual awakening and great Christian revivals in the days of

137

Martin Luther and John and Charles Wesley. But those foundations have crumbled and Europe is now in a post-Christian era. In England, less than 5 percent of the population attend church regularly. Here in America, the foundations of biblical faith, which helped to build a strong nation, are under heavy attack; and the damage is already extensive. Nowhere has the damage seemed to be greater than in the area of the so-called healing arts, as we shall see.

Shirley MacLaine and Edgar Cayce

The massive effort of the Planetary Commission in 1986 to draw millions of people unwittingly into New Age theology through their year-end meditation was only the beginning. The next major event came just a few weeks later when the ABC television network aired a mini-series (18-19 January 1987) on Shirley MacLaine's personal spiritual adventure, *Out On A Limb*. During this five-hour odyssey, the viewing audience was introduced to concepts of reincarnation, trance channeling (contact with demonic spirits), legends of Atlantis, extraterrestrials, yoga, meditation and astral projection (out-of-body experiences). Through this one endeavor alone, millions of people in search of spiritual reality were given a counterfeit answer. The only prerequisite for accepting this answer is to reject the reality of Satan, personal sin, and a personal God, apart from ourselves, to whom we are accountable. To a me-oriented, "if it feels good, do it" generation, this answer is like frosting on the cake.

Shirley MacLaine did not stop with her television special. She also planned to help thousands more to "get in touch with their Higher Self" through a series of seminars, scheduled for every major city in the country, starting with Virginia Beach, Virginia. Why Virginia Beach? Because it is the home of the Association for Research and Enlightenment (ARE), the institution dedicated to preserving the teachings and "readings" of Edgar Cayce, sometimes referred to as the Sleeping Prophet.

The teachings of Edgar Cayce and his present-day association were instrumental in Shirley's quest to "find her true self." She, like thousands of other seekers, was led into the world of the occult through the books promoted by the ARE. She states in the ARE January 1987 newsletter, "As I read about Edgar Cayce and his 'psychic readings,' I found myself fascinated with the idea that they might be true and certainly a good set of life values for consideration." Titles included in ARE's 1987 Annual Bookstore Edition include: *Numerology and the Divine Triangle, Pyramid Power, Cosmic Crystals: Crystal Consciousness and the New Age, A Vision of the Aquarian Age, Gods in the Making,* and *The Goddesses in Every Woman.* Of course, they also feature books by Shirley MacLaine, Carl Jung and John Randolph Price. So it is only natural that Shirley would want to honor this organization by launching her New Age proselytizing tour at the home of the greatest promoter of New Age metaphysics of modern times.

Born in Hopkinsville, Kentucky, in 1877, Cayce claimed to have played with "spirit children" at the age of seven and entered his first trance state at the age of twenty. Without any medical training, he gave 14,246 "readings" while in a trance state. Most of these involved medical diagnosis and advice. Other topics discussed in these trances (altered states of consciousness) were reincarnation, aura charts, psychic phenomena, Atlantis, prehistoric Egypt, spiritism and numerology. Thus began the modern marriage of holistic health to the world of the occult.

Holistic Health

Today's fast-paced, stressful way of life has produced a nation of fast-food consumers with incredibly poor and lazy health habits. The recent emphasis on preventative medicine, personal health responsibility, exercise, less reliance on drugs and treating the whole person are welcome and badly needed changes. Unfortunately, holistic health concepts don't stop there.

One of man's chief concerns down through the ages has been his own health, along with the fear of death. So it is only natural that the forces of deception would try to make their influence felt in these vital areas. Reincarnation, for example, offers man the false hope of many lives after death, insulating him against any fear of judgment. This belief is fast becoming America's "new religion." According to a *U.S.A. Today* poll conducted the week prior to the airing of Shirley MacLaine's mini-series, 23 percent of Americans believed in reincarnation.[1] This was nearly a decade ago. The percentage would probably be even higher today.

However, the area which is unsuspectedly touching people with New Age practices more than any other is holistic health, sometimes known as the "new medicine." This erosion of a once solid scientific medical foundation has happened through a new definition of the word "energy." In the past, we have thought of human energy as meaning that which results from proper sleep, good nutrition and an absence of sickness or disease. Today's definition in holistic health circles involves more than that. It involves one's concept of spiritual truth.

Redefining Energy

The pantheistic or New Age view of spiritual truth is that God is simply the sum total of all creation, the "life force" which flows through all living things. Therefore, New Agers believe, this life force flows through our bodies as well and determines our state of health. Many promoters of holistic health see most of our problems as resulting from the misalignment of the latent, but scientifically undetectable, energy within the body. This is not gravitational, electromagnetic or nuclear energy. It is not an energy that can be measured or monitored in the physical world. Instead, it appears to be a "spiritual" force which can only be explained through a pantheistic/

occult belief system and, interestingly enough, only seems to work for those who have faith in, or submit themselves to, this system.

To restore good health, thousands of people in this country are now submitting themselves to practices based upon this Eastern view of the nature of God, which states that "all is one and connected" through a mystical divine energy. If this were true, the implication is that man is not separated from God and therefore is not in need of salvation. Dr. Harold Bloomfield, a promoter of transcendental meditation, while addressing the 1978 Holistic Health Conference in San Diego stated, "In your essential nature you are divine and that's a major focus of our holistic health movement."[2] In line with this, the Association of Holistic Health defines itself as "becoming aware of higher levels of consciousness."[3] In this system of thought, there is no creature-Creator distinction; all manifestations of power are godly; and the mind is divine and potentially omnipotent. What a perfect cover for the activity of demonic power in these last days.

The chakra centers of yoga and the meridians of acupuncture are an excellent example of this energy flow concept. The energy flow of acupuncture is referred to as "chi" and involves the interplay of yin and yang. These are the supposed opposite forces of nature which produce day-night, summer-winter, sun-moon, male-female polarities. According to this theory, yin and yang circulate in the body from organ to organ along invisible meridians. It is believed that disease results when the body's energy flow becomes unbalanced or blocked. By inserting long, very fine needles into specific spots, this energy flow is allegedly influenced and balanced.

Thus, the underlying philosophy of this practice is spiritual, not physiological. The question Christians should be asking themselves is not "Does this seem to work?" but rather, "What are the long-term, spiritual consequences of this practice?" This basic idea of a mystical, nonphysical energy, which somehow unites man with the cosmos, is central not only to acupuncture, but also to polarity therapy, applied kinesiology, yoga, homeopathy, Reichian therapy, reflexology and iridology. The fact that we can never quite explain how these nontraditional therapies work always comes back to the fact that they are so closely connected to this elusive energy force. Let's use *iridology* as an example.

Iridology

Iridology has become one of the most popular techniques used in holistic circles. There are well over twelve thousand practitioners of iridology in the United States today. This form of eye diagnosis can be traced back to astrology and originated in China.

Iridology is the diagnosis of the state of the physical body through the condition of the iris. It seems to offer a combination of pseudoscience and the occult, depending upon the practitioner's world view. It should be understood that a person doesn't necessarily have to be involved in the occult to believe in certain aspects of iridology. A small percentage of practitioners, some of whom I personally know, are simply convinced that certain diseases can be detected by various reactions they produce in the iris, which can be identified by a trained eye. This may explain why the practice has gained some acceptance in Christian circles. Nevertheless people are becoming involved in this practice without taking a close look at the philosophy behind it.

Dr. Bernard Jensen, a naturopath-chiropractor from Los Angeles, is considered the leading authority on iridology. Many conventional physicians, however, are being attracted to this form of diagnosis as well, particularly those with metaphysical leanings. The first scientific studies on this subject were reported in the 28 September 1979, issue of the *Journal of the American Medical Association*. Dr. Jensen was one of three iridologists involved in the study. The test dealt with detection of kidney disease. In this study, one iridologist correctly identified only 26 percent of the patients undergoing dialysis as having kidney disease.

As mentioned, some practitioners sincerely believe that iridology is a legitimate form of diagnosis, but many use it "mediumistically" rather than medically. In this way, the eye serves as a point of contact, in much the same way as the hand does in fortunetelling. In cases such as this, eye diagnosis can be very successful. In fact, some people with practically no medical training have diagnosed illnesses with great accuracy.

Counterfeit Miracles

It is most unwise to accept some new technique simply because it seems to work. We need to look at the philosophy behind the technique and remember that the attraction of the occult is that it often does work, at least temporarily. Our tendency is to underestimate the power of Satan, including his ability to perform miracles. We forget that when Moses stood before Pharaoh, Pharaoh's magicians and occultists were able to duplicate, in succession, each of the miracles which God performed through Moses, up to a point. Some of these duplications may have actually been illusions, but others were quite possibly real miracles performed through demonic powers.

Scripture tells us in 2 Thessalonians 2:9-10a (NIV) that, "The coming of the lawless one will be in accordance with the work of Satan displayed in all kinds of counterfeit miracles, signs and wonders, and in every sort of evil that deceives those who are perishing." The word "counterfeit" in this passage is often misinterpreted to mean something which is not really happening but only appears to be happening to the naked eye, such as an act of illusion. However, the term "counterfeit" in the above context does not imply an illusion but refers instead to a miracle of demonic origin whose source is evil. Such miracles, although very real are not of God and in this respect are considered counterfeit.

God performs miracles for the good of His people, to uphold truth and to bring glory to His name. Satan, on the other hand, performs miracles to further deceive and enslave those who refuse to accept the truth. He always has ulterior motives which prompt his actions, motives which are aimed at lifting himself above God. Discernment is needed to distinguish between the two.

God's miracles (including the healing of illnesses) usually occur in response to our simple heartfelt prayers, accompanied by a simple faith—our belief that God truly hears us when we pray in the name of Jesus Christ. It is God's own awesome supernatural power that heals us according to His will. Satan's miracles, on the other hand, usually result when people go into altered states and/or try to manipulate "energy," which has the affect of summoning demonic entities; giving them a license to come through and perform the healing.

I am convinced that most practitioners of the occult are unaware of the fact that this so-called life force or energy is actually nothing more than demonic spirits manifesting their limited power. Most people involved in the occult would probably cease their practices if they really understood this fact. However, the belief in a mysterious force of nature that can somehow be tapped into is a much more pleasant and acceptable explanation for the existence of this energy.

Occult-based Medicine

A close look at the thousands of holistic health centers around this country will reveal that they teach a variety of questionable practices such as past-life regression, astrology, sensory isolation, induced altered states of consciousness, American Native shamanism (another name for witch-doctoring), hypnosis and various forms of divination (such as the Tarot and *I Ching*).

An excellent example of this is Boulder College in Boulder, Colorado. This is a school that offers credit courses in the healing arts. Course offerings include: Jung and the Evolution of Mythology, Tarot, Fundamentals of Holistic Health, Iridology, Transpersonal Astrology, Oriental Herbology, Death as a Spiritual Teacher, Fundamentals of Nutrition, Symbolic Aspects of *I Ching*, Nutritional Biochemistry and Stress Management. This hodgepodge curriculum of health and occult boasts a faculty of twelve master's degrees and seven Ph.D.'s, one with a Ph.D. in biomedical engineering from Massachusetts Institute of Technology.

Another example of this marriage of the occult to holistic health practices can be found in a program guide to the Whole Life Expo, a conference that was held at the Marriott Hotel in Boston on 31 January through 2 February 1986. Workshops offered at this conference included: Pioneering a New Planetary Perspective, Using Media as a Tool for Social Change, The Spiritual Heritage and Destiny of America,

Health Forces: The Art and Cultivation of Human Energy, Love Is Power: Gaining Self-Awareness through the Insight of a Trance Medium, Rebirthing and Therapeutic Touch, and Ecstasy in Marriage: A Spiritual Technology Deeply and Directly into Your Higher Self. The conference also abounded with workshops on acupuncture, iridology, astrology, relaxation through meditation techniques and trance channeling (as demonstrated by Kevin Ryerson in *Out On A Limb*).

Whole Life Expo featured programs with doctors from Harvard Medical School and Johns Hopkins University. It is obvious that occult-based medicine is no longer on the fringes but has made major gains in blending with traditional medical practices.

Gaining Acceptance

The Catholic Health Association of the United States 1986 Achievement Citation went to St. Mary's Hospital and Health Center in Tucson, Arizona. The award was presented to the hospital for their "integration of Traditional Indian Medicine into today's health system." A conference, emphasizing the spiritual focus of the healing process for all people, was offered at the hospital on 9-16 January 1987. Their brochure states, "Participants learn from Traditional Medicine people, increasing their awareness and expansion of consciousness through experiential learning to develop a sensitive, spiritual approach to the healing process."[4]

The word "spirituality" is very popular in New Age circles. People need to be aware that there is a vast difference between New Age spirituality and the biblical meaning of this word. The contrast is evident in an article by Lawrence Le Shan, Ph.D. in *A Science of Mind* magazine. In describing holistic medicine, he states,

> Interestingly enough, holistic medicine has come to a very clear and practical definition of "spiritual" . . . It means such very hard disciplines as prayer and meditation, that bring you to those moments where you really know 'I am one with the cosmos.' You know that we are all parts of the universe, that we stand on the bedrock of the universe, and that our isolation, loneliness and alienation are in large part illusion.[5]

A study of UFO contacts reveals this same "cosmic gospel." The message from these supposedly benevolent beings is one of a coming New Age, expanded human potential and a new avatar to show us the way. In New Age theology, Jesus is recognized and honored, but only as one in a succession of avatars who came to bring enlightenment. In this way they attempt to explain away the uniqueness of Christ. By contrast, the Scriptures tell us,

> He . . . seated Him [Christ] at His right hand in the heavenly places, far above all rule and authority and power and dominion, and every name that is named, not only in this age, but also in the one to come. (Eph. 1:20-21, NAS)

Dr. Le Shan has taught classes at the Oasis Center (Chicago), a New Age awareness center with programs which reach out into the surrounding community. Another center of this type is the Stress Reduction and Learning Center in my home state of Indiana. The center, located in Ft. Wayne, features a New Age bookstore, sensory isolation tanks which are designed to take the brain to the trance-inducing alpha wave level, and classes in the energies of ancient music, Folklore, Herbs and Magic, Kinship with all Life and Energy Transfer: A Therapeutic Touch Process. This last class has been taught by Myra Till, a locally popular registered nurse. A description of this class informs potential students that

> the main goal of the course is for you to become aware of your own energies, the energy that is both within and beyond the boundaries of your skin. You will learn to direct these energies to another person in aiding them to move into profound states of relaxation and pain management.[6] We will explore the process of energy transfer with one's hands, eyes, voice, and presence.[7]

Myra Till lectures throughout the state and writes articles for *Beginnings: A Newsletter of the American Holistic Nursing Association.* She was awarded the Indiana Nurse of the Year Award in 1986. She is also director of all school nurses for Fort Wayne Community Schools and worked with a former governor of Indiana in setting up guidelines for school nurses throughout the state.

Our children might be getting more than conventional medical treatment when they report to the office due to an injury during recess or an upset stomach.

Even the Girl Scout program is not exempt from these influences. On page 66 of the *Girl Scout Badges and Signs* book, the yin/yang symbol is used to represent the World in My Community proficiency badge. In the *Junior Girl Scout Handbook*, yoga exercises are explained. The theme for their 1987 program was "The Year of Magic." We are past the day when one had to join a cult or seek out a "guru" to be influenced by these unorthodox spiritual practices. Instead, the problem now is trying to avoid them.

In addition to those already mentioned, there are hundreds of other New Age/holistic organizations located throughout the United States, many of which are connected. A study center in Big Sur, California, known as Esalen, is probably the most well known New Age center in the country. In a section of the *Aquarian Conspiracy* entitled "California and the Aquarian Conspiracy," Marilyn Ferguson stated,

> In the 1950s and 1960s, Aldous Huxley was among those who encouraged Michael Murphy and Richard Price in their 1961 decision to open Esalen, the residential center in California's Big Sur area that helped mid-wife much of what came to be known as the human-potential movement . . . a human potential movement would help break down the barriers between mind and body, between Eastern wisdom and Western action, between

individuals and society, and thus between the
limited self and the potential self.[8]

Seminar leaders at Esalen have included Carl
Rogers and Abraham Maslow, well-known psychologist Rollo May, author Carlos Castaneda,
Zen enthusiast Allen Watts (formerly an Episco-
pal priest), B.F. Skinner, Jean Houston, Norman
Cousins and Fritz Perls. California, New York
City and the Denver-Boulder, Colorado area
seem to be the main centers of New Age activity. From these areas, this activity spreads to the
rest of the country.

In *Psychic Healing*, an excellent book on the
occult influence in holistic health, authors John
Weldon and Zola Levitt tell of another similar
center also located in California.

> The famous authority on death and dying,
> Dr. Elizabeth Kubler-Ross, is another example
> of how even professionals can become
> occulticly involved. A psychic-healing advocate,
> she currently has about five spirit-guides ("Sa-
> lem" is her favorite) . . . at her Shantih Nilaya
> retreat center in California (where psychic
> healing and spiritism work hand in hand).[9]

A Spiritual Battle

If we think that by hard work we can make
the New Age movement go away and if that is
our only goal, we will quickly lose heart. Yet we
are called by Jesus to be salt and light. There is
no need for salt to preserve unless something
would go rotten without its presence. There is
no need of light if there is no darkness for it to
penetrate.

The nature of the spiritual battle in which we find ourselves can be clearly seen in statements made pertaining to the medical profession by Donald Keys, president of Planetary Citizens, in his book, *Earth at Omega.*

> The world needs large numbers of constructive social-change persons who can stand strongly as the old order crashes down about them causing dismay and pessimism in the minds and lives of those who lack vision and who do not understand the nature of the transition . . . Transformative infiltration is proving valuable notably within the medical profession.[10]

I believe that competent physicians and sound medical practices are a blessing from God. I also believe that we can look to His Word for guiding principles to lead a physically and spiritually healthy life. Proverbs 4:20-22 says, "My son, attend to my words; incline thine ear unto my sayings. Let them not depart from thine eyes; keep them in the midst of thine heart. For they are life unto those that find them, and health to all their flesh."

Occultists, on the other hand, have always sought to avoid the results of man's fall into sin by trying to control nature, human abilities and death. The forces of darkness are only too willing to accommodate these people, leading them to believe that they are actually in control. This is why involvement in the occult is forbidden so many times in Scripture. It means direct contact with forces which are alien and hostile to both

God and man. One of many biblical warnings is found in Deuteronomy 18:10-12a:

> There shall not be found among you any one that maketh his son or his daughter to pass through the fire, or that useth divination, or an observer of times, or an enchanter, or a witch, Or a charmer, or a consulter with familiar spirits, or a wizard, or a necromancer. For all that do these things are an abomination unto the Lord.

A strongly anti-Christian newspaper, published by reincarnationist Dick Sutphen, who has appeared on "The Phil Donahue Show" and conducted seminars reaching thousands of people, reveals the overall hostile and deceptive nature of this end-time battle. The paper is called *What Is–New Age Activists* and boasts,

> One of the biggest advantages we have as New Agers is, once the occult, metaphysical and New Age terminology is removed, we have concepts and techniques that are very acceptable to the general public. So we can change the names and demonstrate the power. In so doing, we open the New Age door to millions who normally would not be receptive. On the other hand, the Born-Again Christians, our most vocal antagonists, relate everything back to the blood of Christ and to the Bible . . . But our momentum will become so great that the combined efforts of all antagonists can't stop us unless they do so politically. Laws are the only way to block the New Age movement from growing within the consciousness of our population . . . New Age Activists encourage you as an individual to

network with your family, friends, and associates, and to infuse New Age concepts and awareness into every area of your personal world, from the office to the bridge club, from the schoolroom to the Little League.[11]

It is clear from this and previous statements that New Agers have an agenda. They intend to penetrate and permeate every segment of society with their occult beliefs—including the field of medicine. And, they are not planning to go away! They will continue their pursuit until their goal of a New World Order has been achieved—and the "problem" of Christianity has been eliminated.

Conclusion

We have examined in these four chapters the lives and beliefs of some of this century's top New Agers along with the events that they helped set in motion. I believe we can safely conclude from the evidence presented that individuals such as Helena Blavatsky and Alice Bailey could not possibly have been divinely inspired. Their rebellious personal lives and direct involvement in the occult made them perfect vessels for use by the master deceiver, not by God.

We have seen how their pantheistic ideas have permeated American society and how the occult concepts of divine energy, spirit guides, altered states of consciousness, and belief in a cosmic Christ have become fashionable. Consequently, our society seems to be in greater disarray today than ever. The world, I believe, has become a worse, not a better, place as a result of this growing occult influence. Yet, in spite of this fact, the New World Order is being built on this very foundation.

Organizations such as the Theosophical Society, Lucis Trust, World Goodwill, and other Blavatsky/Bailey creations operating at the heart of today's New Age movement, have gained considerable influence. However, whether or not they serve as the main power base for the emerging world government is debatable. Most of the leaders of these hard-core New Age organizations, I discovered, also belong to other, seemingly more powerful organizations with a more broad and direct political influence, such as the Masonic Lodge (Freemasonry). Blavatsky and Bailey, as we have seen, were no exception as they were both high-level female Masons.

Although I personally believe it is impossible for one organization, such as the Masonic Lodge, to single-handedly mastermind and manage all the details of an international conspiracy to create a world government, it is more than evident that a large network of organizations with a common mindset exists and that they are collaborating to bring about certain end results. These groups appear to share certain values (or lack of values) and are held together by a common pursuit—the ushering in of a New Age of global peace and prosperity in which man becomes divine (gods) and occult principles govern the world.

This network is composed of the secret societies, hundreds of quasi-secret occult organizations (which the secret societies seem to influence), and a multitude of idealistic groups that have naively joined the cause in pursuit of world peace, or to help solve other "world problems." Within this movement, certain organizations, for whatever reasons, have become more powerful than others. At the risk of oversimplifying, I will attempt to summarize how this network of organizations functions and interrelates.

The inner circle of the New Age movement (in Western society) seems to consist of individuals from the highest levels of Freemasonry, along with important members of other slightly less powerful "policy making" groups such as the Club of Rome, the Council on Foreign Relations, and the Trilateral Commission (whose leaders are often closely connected with, or are themselves members of, the Masonic Institution). These so-called round-table groups are closely tied to the United Nations and receive much of their funding from various international financiers who are also part of the Masonic network.*

Lucis Trust and its immediate network of organizations, on the other hand, seem to be the main link between the secret societies of Freemasonry and the public, serving as a type of "go between." Their purpose, as I see it, has been to prepare the way for the New World

---

*According to World Book Encyclopedia-1986 Edition, more than one hundred organizations maintain a special relationship with Freemasonry (see *En Route To Global Occupation*, p. 92).

Order, by conditioning the masses to accept its "spiritual" principles. (It only makes sense. If a world government was ever to take place, it would have to go public at some point; it could not be kept secret forever.) The process of conditioning society has been going on for about one hundred years, but it has greatly intensified during the last generation. Exposing this conditioning process has been the main focus of my book.

As a result of the combined efforts of these and other similar groups, what was once secret information—contained within the innermost chambers of Freemasonry—is now out in the open. Information on how to tap into the occult by achieving a trance state, for example, can today be obtained in any major bookstore. This was not the case only thirty years ago. Lucis Trust and its network of organizations, more than any other group, have borne responsibility for popularizing these once arcane teachings of the secret societies (which are, in fact, the same basic beliefs taught by the leaders of Buddhism and Hinduism in the Far East). In pantheistic countries, such as India, Tibet, and Thailand, occult information has been accessible to the public for centuries; but the "Christian-based" countries of Western society had to be specially conditioned and prepared before they would embrace the occult concepts of the New Age.

Another group of organizations has been involved in laying the "political" groundwork for public acceptance of the coming world order.

They are part of a cleverly disguised effort to make Americans believe that "we the people" are actually the ones in control of this "unprecedented" move toward "world peace and unity." These societies are trying to create the impression that they are just part of a growing democratic grassroots movement. Organizations in this group include the World Federalist Association, the World Future Society, the World Constitution and Parliament Association, Planetary Citizens, World Union, and One World, to name just a few. Some of the leaders of these organizations are directly associated with Lucis Trust or its spin-off groups; some of them are also high-level Freemasons.

The outer, more visible tier of organizations in this network consists of groups such as Green Peace, the Rainbow Coalition, and the World Council of Churches. While some of the leaders of these organizations are directly involved in the world government movement, most of their members are well-meaning people who are largely unaware of the real motivation and intention of those above them. They simply want to be involved in supporting "humanitarian," "social," or "environmental" organizations which they are convinced are helping to improve world conditions.

If we are to believe New Agers such as Alice Bailey and others reviewed in this book, individuals at the higher levels of this movement hear directly from the Ascended Masters. As preposterous as this may sound to the average person, if leaders in the secret societies are in fact hearing from the supernatural realm, I can assure you it is not Ascended Masters that they are communicating with. Rather, they are receiving instructions directly from demonic entities—fallen angels—who seem to be guiding this entire initiative along. If this is true, then the "Grand Architect" of this diabolic endeavor is none other than Lucifer himself.

This undertaking then is not a conspiracy of any one organization plotting to take over the world. Yet it is a "type" of conspiracy—a Satanically inspired effort with Lucifer, or Satan, at the helm. If one is a Christian, this knowledge should not come as a surprise, since Christians believe, according to the Bible, that Satan and his angels have been warring against God and His angels ever since their fall. The fact is, Satan has been a liar, deceiver, and conspirator from the beginning. First, he conspired against God with a third of the angels, wanting to be God himself. Then, he conspired against God by deceiving the first humans, Adam and Eve, into disobeying Him.

Today we are witnessing the final stages of this unique endeavor. Satan wants a world government, complete with a world religion, so that he can enslave humanity and receive the worship of man. At stake is his ego—and our souls. Based on world events of the last five years, it has become readily apparent that this effort is rapidly reaching a climax.

Only a few questions remain, such as: How much time do we have left? Will it take a major crisis in Bosnia, the Middle-East, or somewhere else to bring the world to its knees, or can the "hierarchy" seduce mankind into accepting the New World Order peacefully? Will the occult World Order be falsely introduced in the name of Christ? What will happen to Christians? Will they be raptured before the most intense persecution begins? God alone knows the answers to these questions. However, I do know the following.

There is a deep spiritual hunger in the world today that New Age mysticism, Buddhism, and all the other "isms" have not been able to meet. The only way that hunger can be met is by spending time with the one who placed that hunger within us in the first place. Our spiritual survival in the days ahead will depend upon the closeness of our walk with Him.

Jesus claimed to be the Good Shepherd and said that His sheep knew Him and knew His voice. Those in positions of spiritual leadership in the New Age movement, on the other hand, are receiving their marching orders while in altered states of consciousness, from their spirit guides or so-called higher selves. Thus, the world system, composed of all those who are not allowing themselves to be guided by the Holy Spirit, are being led down a path that the very demons of hell want humanity to follow. From Madame Blavatsky to Chardin, and now through people like Robert Muller, John Price, and Barbara Marx Hubbard, humanity is being led to its "Omega Point of deception, destruction and darkness."

In Matthew 7:24-27, Jesus spoke of two different groups of people. One group was called wise because they built their house upon the foundation of His words. The other group foolishly built upon a foundation of their own making. Spiritual storms are being unleashed upon this world, and "our house" will stand or fall, depending upon our foundation. We can choose to trust in ourselves and our own human potential, or we can choose to stand on "the Rock of Ages"; the God of Abraham, Isaac, and Jacob; the one who said, "I am the light of the world" (John 8:12).

God's pattern as recorded over and over again in the Bible is: Warning, warning, warning, and then finally judgment. He is not willing that any should perish, but that all should come to repentance. However, judgment against the ungodly finally comes, and when it does, it does so swiftly. To all those who are following a "metaphysical gospel" I would say, leave the "quest," turn from "the path," which is in reality the broad road that leads to destruction. Come to the cross where Jesus said, "It is finished"— paid in full.

If you have never accepted Jesus Christ as your Savior but would like to do so, here is what you must do:

First of all, you must understand what it is that God has done for you through Jesus Christ. John 3:16 explains:

> For God so loved the world, that he gave his only begotten Son, that whosoever believeth in him should not perish, but have everlasting life.

God sent his son to die in our place, so that we might be saved from the penalty of our sins. Had we been perfect, this would not have been necessary; we could have entered Heaven on our own merits. But, this is not the case.

> For all have sinned, and come short of the glory of God. (Rom. 3:23)

The "gift" of salvation (Rom. 6:23) is available only through Jesus Christ, because He is the only one who, as a perfect being—God in the flesh—was able to pay the necessary price for our sins. It took a perfect sacrifice to overcome Satan's claim to our souls.

> Jesus saith unto him, "I am the way, the truth, and the life: no man cometh unto the Father, but by me." (John 14:6)

> For there is one God, and one mediator between God and men, the man Christ Jesus; Who gave himself a ransom for all, to be testified in due time. (I Tim. 2:5-6; also read John 3:36 and Acts 4:12)

If Jesus is man's only hope for eternal life, and if we are unable to earn this gift, then what must we do to receive it? We must accept the fact that Jesus paid the penalty for our sins and believe that we have eternal life as a result of what he did. It's that simple!

> Yet to all who received him, to those who believed in his name, he gave the right to become children of God. (John 1:12 [NIV])

> He that believeth on him is not condemned: but he that believeth not is condemned already, because he hath not believed in the name of the only begotten Son of God. (John 3:18)

If you sincerely wish to accept the gift of eternal life through Jesus Christ, simply pray to God in your own words. Do it right now. Confess to him that you are a sinner and would like to be forgiven. Tell Him that you accept His Son, Jesus Christ, and that you believe His sacrifice on the cross was sufficient to cover your sins. Thank God for what He has done, and ask Him to help you live the kind of life that would be pleasing to Him. *God will hear your prayer if it comes from a sincere heart!*

If you have just accepted Jesus as Lord, you now have eternal life. Satan no longer has a claim to your soul. You are at peace with God and have entered into a permanent relationship with Him. The quality of this relationship, however, is up to you. Please allow God to take "complete" control of your life!

If you are already a Christian, here are some words of advice and encouragement:

1. Stand firm.

The Apostle Paul, in his letter to the Corinthians, wrote:

> Be on guard; stand firm in the faith; be men
> of courage; be strong. . . . Let nothing move
> you. Always give yourselves fully to the work
> of the Lord. (I Cor. 16:13a, 15:58a [NIV])

Paul's exhortations to the church in Corinth still apply to us today. Just because it appears as if an anti-Christian world government is imminent does not mean that we should help bring it about by "throwing in the towel" and doing nothing. As mentioned earlier in this book, we must raise a standard, while proclaiming the truth of Jesus Christ for the sake of those who will listen. It is because so few people are speaking out to warn others, that the New Age movement is making such progress in these days. As James emphasized, "Faith without works is dead" (James 2:26). There is much work to be done!

• Inform people at your church about the deceptive teachings of the New Age; as many of the false doctrines of pantheism and the occult are now subtly making their way into some of our churches, often cloaked under the banner of Christianity.

• Be involved in your schools. Examine new curricula and fight for change where needed. You may be surprised at what your son or daughter is learning.

• Share the truth about the current world situation with members of your family and with friends and neighbors. Keep them posted of important developments while being a positive Christian example with your life.

• Pray for the salvation of unsaved loved ones and tactfully share the message of Christ with them. Your faithful words may determine their eternal destiny.

• Pray for your elected officials. There are still a few good people in government trying to hold back the tide. They need your prayers and encouragement, which brings me to my next point.

Get involved politically. As New Age writer Dick Sutphen revealed earlier, occultists do not want Christians to be politically active. They fear that their momentum could be slowed and their efforts diminished, or even temporarily stopped, if Christians ever got seriously involved in standing against the New World Order. This knowledge alone should provide enough incentive for us to do whatever possible to "stand in the gap" politically. Here are some things you can do:

• Write or call your elected officials, expressing where you stand on important issues. Urge them to introduce, or vote in favor of, legislation defending our national sovereignty and our Constitutional freedoms, while opposing legislation that threatens Christian values. Do not underestimate your influence in this area.

• Sponsor church or community petition drives, when necessary, to communicate the seriousness of your concerns. Personally deliver your signed petitions to the office of the elected official whose attention you are trying to get.

• Consider running for office yourself. There are not enough concerned Christians with a voice in government. You will never know if you can win unless you try.

While it is important to be politically active, we must stand firm spiritually as well. It takes both spiritual preparedness and physical action to live a life that is pleasing to God. Therefore, be consistent in your walk with the Lord. Spend time with Him daily by praying (talking) to Him and reading His Word (the Bible).

2. Maintain a sense of urgency.

There are two ways to respond to the information contained in this book. One is to panic and become overwhelmed; the other is to allow it to instill in us a sense of urgency. This second reaction is God's desire for us. Reflecting on the urgency of life, someone once said, "You should treat every day as if it's your last one, because one of these days you're going to be right." The fact is, we will not be on this earth forever, so we must do what we can with the time that we *do* have.

As a reminder of the relentless nature of the battle and the brevity of time, we just recently received word that something known as the Philadelphia II Initiative is being introduced in the state of Washington. This initiative calls for the holding of a worldwide constitutional convention to introduce a world constitution (for a world government). It is being sponsored by a former two-term United States Senator, Mike Gravel, who is also the director of One World. Although he failed to get a similar initiative on

ballots in Missouri and California last year, he is
determined to push ahead, believing that his
perseverance will eventually overcome any remaining obstacles. Gravel's effort, which has
received strong support from the World Federalist Association, is only one more example of
the one-world movement "going public." (Things
keep moving right along!)

While some Christians feel like panicking because of developments such as these, others,
strangely enough, are becoming complacent due
to overconfidence in our political process. Because of the results of recent elections which
placed a number of conservative, pro-Constitu-
tion Christians in Congress, some people
wrongly believe that we have nothing to be
concerned about and that we have all the time
in the world. The fact is, the globalist agenda, in
the past, has continued to make progress, even
during conservative administrations.

Therefore, I would caution Christians reading this book not to make the mistake of becoming complacent. Rather, stay focused on
doing God's will. This means taking a stand both
politically *and* spiritually. Millions of people need
to be reached with the hope of Jesus Christ.
Their souls are at stake—and time may be much
shorter than any of us realize.

> And do this, understanding the present time.
> The hour has come for you to wake up from
> your slumber, because our salvation is nearer
> now than when we first believed. The night is
> nearly over; the day is almost here. So let us

put aside the deeds of darkness and put on
the armor of light. (Rom. 13:11-12 [NIV])

3. Don't lose hope.

The Word of God offers us tremendous encouragement and hope. Regardless of whether
Christians are raptured (suddenly taken out of
this world to be with God) prior to the start of
the "Great Tribulation," in the middle of it, or
at the end (at the actual second coming of Jesus
Christ), we know that any suffering in this world
will be short-lived. It will not continue indefi-
nitely. Paul assures us of this fact in 2
Thessalonians 2:8, where he describes the glori-
ous return of Jesus, along with the destiny of
the Satanic world ruler and his kingdom:

> And then the lawless one will be revealed,
> whom the Lord Jesus will overthrow with the
> breath of his mouth and destroy by the splen-
> dor of his coming. (NIV)

However, even if we do face death as a result of physical persecution, we can take comfort in knowing that we have an incredible eternity ahead of us. Although Satan can make our
lives difficult and may be responsible for perse-
cuting us in this life, one thing he cannot do is
take away our souls. If we trust Jesus as Lord,
our destiny in heaven has been sealed. No matter what happens to us, in the end, *we win!*

> In all these things we are more than conquer-
> ors through him who loved us. For I am con-
> vinced that neither death nor life, neither
> angels nor demons, neither the present nor

the future, nor any powers, neither height
nor depth, nor anything else in all creation,
will be able to separate us from the love of
God that is in Christ Jesus our Lord. (Rom.
8:37-39 [NIV])

As Christians, therefore, we have great reason for hope. This is not a time for fear. This is
a time for faith and determination! We know
that God is in control and will have the final say.
So let us boldly move forward, proclaiming the
good news of Jesus Christ while time remains.

He which testifieth these things saith,
"Surely I come quickly." Amen.
Even so, come, Lord Jesus.

—Revelation 22:20

Notes

Chapter One

1. Walter Martin, *The Kingdom of the Cults* (Minneapolis: Bethany Fellowship Inc., 1965), 192.

2. Mary K. Neff, *Personal Memoirs of H.P. Blavatsky* (Wheaton, IL: Theosophical Publishing House, 1937), 23.

3. Ibid., 17.

4. John Steinbacher, *The Man, the Mysticism, the Murder* (Greenwich, CT: Impact Publishers, Inc., 1968), 5.

5. Neff, *Personal Memoirs*, 17.

6. Ibid., 33.

7. Ibid., 37.

8. Martin, *The Kingdom of the Cults*, 223.

9. L. W. Rogers, *Elementary Theosophy* (Pasadena, CA: Theological University Press, 1950), 23-25.

10. Helena Patrovna Blavatsky, *Isis Unveiled* (Pasadena, CA: Theosophical University Press, 1950), 341.

11. Ibid., 10.

12. Ibid., 10.

13. Helena Patrovna Blavatsky, *The Secret Doctrine* (Covina, CA: Theosophical University Press, 1925), 53.

14. Ibid., 53.

15. Ibid., 54.

16. Ibid., 82.

17. Joseph J. Carr, *The Twisted Cross* (Lafayette, LA: Huntington House, Inc., 1985), 275.

18. Nevill Drury, *Dictionary of Mysticism and the Occult* (San Francisco: Harper & Row, 1985), 28.

19. Alice Bailey, *Unfinished Autobiography* (Lucis Trust, P.O. Box 722, Cooper Station, N.Y., N.Y. 10276, 1951), 137, 139.

20. Ibid., 80.

21. *The Spiritual Hierarchy* (World Goodwill, 866 United Nations Plaza, Suite 566-7, N.Y., N.Y. 10017, booklet), 3, 4.

22. Ibid., 4.

23. Alice Bailey, *The Externalisation of the Hierarchy* (New York: Lucis Trust, 1957), 519.

24. *The Spiritual Hierarchy*, 9, 10.

25. Bailey, *The Externalisation of the Hierarchy*, 682.

26. Alice A. Bailey, *My Work by the Tibetan* (New York: Lucis Trust, 1943), 2.

27. Bailey, *The Unfinished Autobiography*, 259.

28. Ibid., 123.

29. Ibid., 91.

30. *Thirty Years Work, The Books of Alice A. Bailey and the Tibetan Master Djwhal Khul* (New York: Lucis Trust, booklet), 15.

31. *World Service Through the Power of Thought* (New York: Lucis Trust, booklet).

32. *The Tibetan Master's Work* (The Arcane School, World Goodwill, 866 United Nations Plaza, Suite 566-7, N.Y., N.Y. 10017, booklet), 3, 4.

33. *Thirty Years Work*, 17.

34. Bailey, *The Externalisation of the Hierarchy*, V.

35. Ibid., V.

36. Compiled by: Wilma Leftwich, *A Profile of A Tax-Exempt Foundation* (New York: Lucis Trust, report), 81.

37. *International Unity* (New York: World Goodwill, booklet), 9–11.

38. Ibid., 8, 9.

39. Ibid., 3, 5.

40. Robert Muller, *The School of Ageless Wisdom*, pamphlet (6005 Royaloak Drive, Arlington, TX 76016), 3.

Chapter Two

1. Marilyn Ferguson, *The Aquarian Conspiracy* (Los Angeles: J.P. Tarcher Inc., 1980), 418–420.

2. Barbara Hannah, *Jung: His Life and Work* (New York: G. P. Putnam's Sons, 1976), 22.

3. Carl Jung, *Memories, Dreams, Reflections* (New York: Random House, 1961), 18.

4. Ibid., 15.

5. Nevill Drury, *Dictionary of Mysticism and the Occult* (New York: Harper and Row, 1985), 137.

6. *Personality Theories: An Introduction*, Textbook (Boston: Houghton Mifflin Company, 1979), 112.

7. Ibid., 112, 113.

8. Leo S. Schumacher, *The Truth About Teilhard* (Twin Circle Publishing Company, booklet, 1968), 25.

9. Teilhard de Chardin, *The Future of Man* (San Francisco: Harper & Row Publishers, 1959), 33, 22.

10. Schumacher, *The Truth About Teilhard*, 30, 31.

11. Zbigniew Brzezinski, *Between Two Ages* (New York: Viking Press, 1970), 73.

12. Robert Muller, *New Genesis–Shaping a Global Spirituality* (New York: Doubleday & Company Inc., 1984), 160.

13. Ibid., 164.

14. Ibid., 192.

15. Teilhard de Chardin, *The Stuff of the Universe* (Paris: L'Activation de L'Energie, Editions de Seuil, 1963), 406.

16. Teilhard de Chardin, *The Future of Man*, 188, 189.

17. Teilhard de Chardin, *The Divine Milieu* (San Francisco: Harper & Row Publishers, 1957), 33.

18. Pierre Teilhard de Chardin, *Christianity and Evolution* (Ft. Worth, TX: Harcourt Brace Jovanovich, Inc., 1969), 245.

Chapter Three

1. Winkie Pratney, *Devil Take the Youngest* (Lafayette, LA: Huntington House, Inc., 1985), 25.

2. John Randolph Price, *The Super Beings* (Austin, TX: The Quartus Foundation for Spiritual Research, Inc., 1981), ix.

3. Ibid., x.

4. John Randolph Price, *The Planetary Commission* (Austin, TX: The Quartus Foundation for Spiritual Research, Inc., 1984), 21.

5. Ibid., 28.

6. John Randolph Price, *May Report* (Austin, TX: The Quartus Foundation for Spiritual Research, Inc., 1986).

7. The Quartus Report (A monthly teaching and sharing guide written for members of the international Quartus Society and published by the Quartus Foundation, Boerne, TX, 1986), vol. V, no. 8, 8.

8. Ibid., 1.

9. *January Update on the Planetary Commission* (Austin, TX: Quartus Foundation, January 1987).

10. Ibid.

11. Price, *The Super Beings*, 1.

12. *New Age Activist*, vol. 1, no. 1 (newsletter, Summer 1986), 5.

13. *The Omega Letter*, vol. 1, no. 8 (newsletter, September 1986), 6.

14. *The Forum*, vol. 7, no. 4 (newsletter, August-September 1986), 13.

15. John Randolph Price, *Practical Spirituality* (Austin, TX: The Quartus Foundation for Spiritual Research, 1985), 18-19.

16. *The Quartus Report*, vol. V, no. 8, 1986, 12.

17. *Report From The Planetary Commission* (Austin, TX: The Quartus Foundation for Spiritual Research, 1 May 1986.

18. Ibid.

19. Barbara Marx Hubbard, *Manual for Co-Creators of the Quantum Leap*, 10–11.

20. Barbara Marx Hubbard, *The Book of Co-Creation, Evolutionary Interpretation of the New Testament*, unpublished manuscript (Centreville, VA: New Visions, 1980), viii.

21. Ibid., xi.

22. Ibid., xiii, xiv.

23. Hubbard, *Manual for Co-Creators*, 55–57.

24. Ibid., 101, 95.

25. Ibid., 60–61.

26. Hubbard, *The Evolutionary Journey*, xiv.

27. *Your Thoughts Count*, Issue One (newsletter, The Million Minutes of Peace Appeal, P.O. Box 2492, New York, NY 10163), 1.

28. Patricia Diane Cota-Robles, President, *New Age Study of Humanity's Purpose* (newsletter, 4 March 1987).

29. Harmonic Convergence (P.O. Box 6111, Boulder, Colorado, 80306, mailing of 25 March 1987).

Chapter Four

1. Monica Collins, "Not Some Spaced-Out California Concept," *U.S.A. Today,* 16 January, 1987, 2A.

2. Wilson & Weldon, *Occult Shock and Psychic Forces* (Colorado Springs: Master Books, 1980), 155.

3. Ibid., 157.

4. *Traditional Indian Medicine in Today's Health System* (report, St. Mary's Hospital and Health Center, 1601 W. St. Mary's Road, Tucson, AZ 85745, January 1987).

5. Dr. Lawrence Le Shan, *Science of Mind* (New York: Collier Books, November 1983), 12, 13.

6. *Stress Reduction Newsletter,* Current Seminars, January 1986.

7. *Stress Reduction Newsletter,* January 1987.

8. Ferguson, *Aquarian Conspiracy,* 137–139.

9. John Weldon and Zola Levitt, *Psychic Healing* (Chicago: Moody Press, 1982), 20.

10. Donald Keys, *Earth at Omega* (Bronx, NY: Branden Publishing Co., Inc., 1982), 129, 127.

11. *New Age Activist,* vol. 1, no. 1 (newsletter, Summer 1986).

Index

Romans 1:21-22; 28, 27
Romans 1:21-23, 92
Romans 3:23, 165
Romans 6:23, 165
Romans 8:37-39, 172
I Samuel 8:7, 109
I Thessalonians 5:3, 109
II Thessalonians 2, 51
II Thessalonians 2:10-11, 27
II Thessalonians 2:9-10a, 145
II Thessalonians 2:8, 171
II Timothy 4:3-4, 95
I Timothy 2:5-6, 165
Zephaniah 3:4, 128
Big Sur, California, 151
Billboard Magazine, 112
Birds, 18, 92
Birth, 64, 66, 82, 122, 123
Bismarck, Otto von, 67
Black thoughts, 103
Blavatsky, Helena, 9, 16, 17-27, 29, 33, 39, 42, 75, 76, 157, 158, 163
Bliss, 70
Blood of Jesus, 21, 22, 71, 95, 154
Bloomfield, Harold, 142
Bookstores, 35, 150, 160
Born-again Christians, 154
Bosnia, 163
Boston, 147
Boulder, Colorado, 93, 131, 147, 152
Brahma, 78
Brahma Kumanis World Spiritual Organization, 128

Brain cells, 118
Brain wave activity, 37, 38
Breaking the seals, 123, 124
Bride of Christ, 136
Broadcasting, 105
Brotherhood, 56
Bryn Mawr College, 115
Brzezinski, Zbigniew, 89
Buddhism, 37, 69, 89, 160, 163
Bush, George, 132-33

C
Caddy, Eileen, 128
Cairo, 135
Calendars, 131
California, 29, 152, 170
"California and The Aquarian Conspiracy," 151
Candle lighting ceremonies, 128
Capitalism, 54
Carl Jung Institute, 80, 93
Carr, Joseph, 25
Castaneda, Carlos, 152
Catholic Health Association, 148
Catholic Holy Office, 88
Catholics, 35, 36, 69
Cayce, Edgar, 139-40
Centering techniques, 46
Chakra, 142
Channeling, 29, 30, 31, 44, 57, 76, 121, 138, 148
Chaos, 32
Charmer, 154
Chelas, 19
Chi, 142
Chicago, 150

McNichols Arena, 106
Magic, 82
Magnetic field, 104, 118
Man, 24, 31, 62, 75, 94,
    101, 109, 126, 134,
    154, 162, 164
  collective thought, 129
  communication with
    God, 47-48
  and consciousness, 90,
    91-92, 104
  created perfect, 96
  creating religions, 95
  daughters of, 40
  Divine Plan for, 30, 32
  and energy, 49
  evolution of, 93, 119,
    121
  goals of, 11-12
  as God, 20-21, 23, 34,
    56, 58, 59, 72, 86,
    100, 101, 106, 122,
    158
  as highly evolved be-
    ings, 33, 68
  Mind Energy, 103
  occult involvement, 40,
    41
  quantum leap, 123, 124
  regeneration of, 63
  saving, 70, 165
  as sinner, 57, 95, 120,
    123
  unification, 94-95
  universal psyche, 83.
    See also Psyche
  and universe, 91
  wickedness of, 65
  and world's resources,
    54

Mankind. See Man
*Manual for Co-Creators of
    the Quantum Leap*
    (Hubbard), 119
Manual for Revolution
    (Blavatsky), 25
Mark of a Saviour, 69-70
Martyrs, 21, 22
Marx, Louis, 115
Mary, 84
Mary's Message to the World
    (Kirkwood), 36
Maslow, Abraham, 152
Masonic Lodge, 27, 41, 42,
    158, 159, 160, 161
Massachusetts Institute of
    Technology, 147
Masters, 19, 20, 22, 25, 26,
    28, 31-33, 43, 48, 50,
    51, 54, 104
Masters of the Wisdom, 32,
    33, 42, 60
Materialism, 60
May, Rollo, 152
Media, 108
Medical diagnosis, 140,
    143-45
Medical profession, 153
Medicine, 140-55
Meditation, 33-38, 46-50,
    93, 104, 110, 114, 129,
    138, 142, 148, 149
Mediums, 18
*Memories, Dreams, Reflec-
    tions* (Jung), 77
Mental plane, 39
Mentor, 125
Meridians, 142
Messiah. See Jesus Christ

*We welcome comments from our
readers. Feel free to write to us at
the following address:*
Editorial Department
Huntington House Publishers
P.O. Box 53788
Lafayette, LA 70505

More Good Books from Huntington House

New World Order:
The Ancient Plan of Secret Societies
by William T. Still

For thousands of years, secret societies have culti-
vated an ancient plan which has powerfully influenced world events. Until now, this secret plan has
remained hidden from view. This book presents
new evidence that a military take-over of the U.S.
was considered by some in the administration of
one of our recent presidents. Although averted, the
forces behind it remain in secretive positions of
power.

ISBN 0-910311-64-1 $8.99

En Route to Global Occupation
by Gary Kah

High-ranking government liaison Gary Kah warns
that national sovereignty will soon be a thing of the
past. Invited to join the WCPA (World Constitution and Parliamentary Association), the author
was involved in the planning and implementation
of a one-world government. For the skeptical ob-
server, the material in this book "should serve as
ample evidence that the drive to create a one-world
government is for real." Reproductions of the
original documentation are included.

ISBN 0-910311-97-8 $9.99

Beyond Political Correctness: Are There Limits to This Lunacy?
by David Thibodaux

Author of the best-selling *Political Correctness: The Cloning of the American Mind,* Dr. David Thibodaux now presents his long awaited sequel—*Beyond Political Correctness: Are There Limits to This Lunacy?* The politically correct movement has now moved beyond college campuses. The movement has succeeded in turning the educational system of this country into a system of indoctrination. Its effect on education was predictable: steadily declining scores on every conceivable test which measures student performance; and, increasing numbers of college freshmen who know a great deal about condoms, homosexuality, and abortion, but whose basic skills in language, math, and science are alarmingly deficient.

ISBN 1-56384-066-9 $9.99

The Dark Side of Freemasonry
Edited by Ed Decker

This book is probably the most significant document ever prepared on the subject of the dark side of the Masonic Lodge. In June 1993, a group of Christian researchers, teachers, and ministry leaders met in Knoxville, Tennessee, to gather together all available information on the subject of Freemasonry and its relationship to the Christian world. Ed Decker brought this explosive material back from Knoxville and here presents it as a warning to those who are unaware of the danger of the Masonic movement.

ISBN 1-56384-061-8 $9.99

Political Correctness:
The Cloning of the American Mind
by David Thibodaux, Ph.D.

The author, a professor of literature at the University of Southwestern Louisiana, confronts head on the movement that is now being called Political Correctness. Political correctness, says Thibodaux, "is an umbrella under which advocates of civil rights, gay and lesbian rights, feminism, and environmental causes have gathered." To incur the wrath of these groups, one only has to disagree with them on political, moral, or social issues. To express traditionally Western concepts in universities today can result in not only ostracism, but even suspension. (According to a recent "McNeil-Lehrer News Hour" report, one student was suspended for discussing the reality of the moral law with an avowed homosexual. He was reinstated only after he apologized.)

ISBN 1-56384-026-X Trade Paper $9.99

The Extermination of Christianity-
A Tyranny of Consensus
by Paul Schenck with Robert L. Schenck

If you are a Christian, you might be shocked to discover that: Popular music, television, and motion pictures are consistently depicting you as a stooge, a hypocrite, a charlatan, a racist, an anti-Semite, or a con artist; you could be expelled from a public high school for giving Christian literature to a classmate; and you could be arrested and jailed for praying on school grounds. This book is a catalogue of anti-Christian propaganda—a record of persecution before it happens!

ISBN 1-56384-051-0 $9.99

Please Tell Me—Questions People Ask
about Freemasonry and the Answers
by Tom C. McKenney

Since the publication of his first book, *The Deadly Deception*, Tom McKenney has appeared on over 200 talk shows, answering tough questions about Freemasonry from viewers and audiences throughout the USA and Canada. Now, in his latest book, McKenney has compiled the questions most often asked by the public concerning the cult-like nature and anti-Christian activities of the Masonic movement. McKenney tackles topics, such as; Masonry's occult roots; Death Oaths and Masonic Execution; Masonry and the Illuminati; and Masonry's opposition to Christian schools. Tom McKenney warns Christians of all denominations to extricate themselves from Masonic movements.

ISBN 1-56384-013-8 $9.99

New Gods for a New Age
by Richmond Odom

There is a new state religion in this country. The gods of this new religion are Man, Animals, and Earth. Its roots are deeply embedded in Hinduism and other Eastern religions. The author of *New Gods for a New Age* contends that this new religion has become entrenched in our public and political institutions and is being aggressively imposed on all of us. This humanistic-evolutionary world view has carried great destruction in its path which can be seen in college classrooms where Christianity is belittled, in the courtroom where good is called evil and evil is called good, and in government where the self-interest of those who wield political power is served as opposed to the common good.

ISBN 1-56384-062-6 $9.99

Can Families Survive in Pagan America?
by Samuel Dresner

Drug addiction, child abuse, divorce, and the welfare state have dealt terrible, pounding blows to the family structure. At the same time, robbery, homicide, and violent assaults have increased at terrifying rates. But, according to the author, we can restore order to our country and our lives. Using the tenets of Jewish family life and faith, Dr. Dresner calls on Americans from every religion and walk of life to band together and make strong, traditional families a personal and national priority again—before it's too late.

ISBN Trade Paper: 1-56384-080-4 $15.99
Hardcover: 1-56384-086-3 $31.99

Out of Control—
Who's Watching Our Child Protection Agencies?
by Brenda Scott

This book of horror stories is true. The deplorable and unauthorized might of Child Protection Services is capable of reaching into and destroying any home in America. No matter how innocent and happy your family may be, you are one accusation away from disaster. Social workers are allowed to violate constitutional rights and often become judge, jury, and executioner. Innocent parents may appear on computer registers and be branded "child abuser" for life. Every year, it is estimated that over 1 million people are falsely accused of child abuse in this country. You could be next, says author and speaker Brenda Scott.

ISBN 1-56384-069-3 $9.99

ORDER THESE HUNTINGTON HOUSE BOOKS !

- America Betrayed—Marlin Maddoux. 7.99
- The Assault—Dale A. Berryhill 9.99
- Beyond Political Correctness—David Thibodaux 9.99
- The Best of HUMAN EVENTS—Edited by James C. Roberts 34.95
- Bleeding Hearts and Propaganda—James R. Spencer 9.99
- Can Families Survive in Pagan America?—Samuel Dresner 15.99
- Circle of Death—Richmond Odom 10.99
- Combat Ready—Lynn Stanley 9.99
- Conservative, American & Jewish—Jacob Neusner 9.99
- The Dark Side of Freemasonry—Ed Decker 9.99
- The Demonic Roots of Globalism—Gary Kah 10.99
- Don't Touch That Dial—Barbara Hattemer & Robert Showers . . . . . 9.99/19.99 HB
- En Route to Global Occupation—Gary Kah 9.99
- Everyday Evangelism—Ray Comfort 10.99
- *Exposing the AIDS Scandal—Dr. Paul Cameron 7.99/2.99
- Freud's War with God—Jack Wright, Jr. 7.99
- Gays & Guns—John Eidsmoe . . . . 7.99/14.99 HB
- Global Bondage—Cliff Kincaid 10.99
- Goddess Earth—Samantha Smith 9.99
- Health Begins in Him—Terry Dorian 9.99
- Heresy Hunters—Jim Spencer 8.99
- Hidden Dangers of the Rainbow—Constance Cumbey 9.99
- High-Voltage Christianity—Michael Brown 10.99
- High on Adventure—Stephen Arrington . . . . :8.99
- Homeless in America—Jeremy Reynalds 9.99
- How to Homeschool (Yes, You!)—Julia Toto 3.99
- Hungry for God—Larry E. Myers 9.99
- I Shot an Elephant in My Pajamas—Morrie Ryskind w/ John Roberts 12.99
- *Inside the New Age Nightmare—Randall Baer 9.99/2.99
- A Jewish Conservative Looks at Pagan America—Don Feder . . . . . 9.99/19.99 HB
- Journey into Darkness—Stephen Arrington 9.99
- Kinsey, Sex and Fraud—Dr. Judith A. Reisman & Edward Eichel 11.99
- The Liberal Contradiction—Dale A. Berryhill 9.99
- Legalized Gambling—John Eidsmoe 7.99
- Loyal Opposition—John Eidsmoe 8.99
- The Media Hates Conservatives—Dale A. Berryhill . . . . 9.99/19.99 HB
- New Gods for a New Age—Richmond Odom 9.99
- One Man, One Woman, One Lifetime—Rabbi Reuven Bulka 7.99
- Out of Control—Brenda Scott . . . . 9.99/19.99 HB
- Outcome-Based Education—Peg Luksik & Pamela Hoffecker 9.99
- The Parched Soul of America—Leslie Kay Hedger w/ Dave Reagan 10.99
- Please Tell Me—Tom McKenney 9.99
- Political Correctness—David Thibodaux 9.99
- Resurrecting the Third Reich—Richard Terrell 9.99
- Revival: Its Principles and Personalities—Winkie Pratney 10.99

*Available in Salt Series

Available at bookstores everywhere or order direct from:
Huntington House Publishers • P.O. Box 53788 • Lafayette, LA 70505
Send check/money order. For faster service use VISA/MASTERCARD.
Call toll-free 1-800-749-4009.
Add: Freight and handling, $3.50 for the first book ordered, and $.50 for
each additional book up to 5 books.